HUSTLING FOR A BUCK

THE ADVENTURE OF LIVING
SELF-EMPLOYED

DAVE GREBER

SPRINGBANK PUBLISHING

Published in 1994 by
Springbank Publishing
5425 Elbow Drive SW
Calgary, Alberta
T2V 1H7

First printing October 1994

Canadian Cataloguing in Publication Data
Greber, Dave, 1950-
Hustling for a buck

ISBN 1-895653-18-5

1. Self-employed. 2. Entrepreneurship. I. Title.
HD8036.G73 1994   338'.04   C94-910860-X

Editor: Gillian Steward
Cover Photo Illustration: Chris Thomas, Tim Lane
Production: DaSilva Graphics Ltd.

Printed and bound in Canada

DISCLAIMER: This book is designed to provide accurate and authoritative information about the subject matter covered.
It is sold with the understanding the author and publisher are not engaged in rendering legal, accounting, or other professional service. If legal or accounting advice, or other expert assistance is required, the services of a competent professional
person should be sought. Oswego College is a product of the author's imagination and is simply the setting for the story.

The stories told here are drawn from information gathered by the author over more than 20 years of writing about people,
their lives, and business. These stories are presented in dramatized and/or fictionalized forms; the only individuals referred
to here by their real names are Dr. Ray Rasker, Henry Zimmer and Herb Cohen.

Acknowledgements

It takes a world of people to ensure one person can complete the work that goes into writing a book. Those I want to acknowledge and thank are:

My family, with love—my mother, my sister Sally Kerr, my brother Harvey, and my sister Lorraine Powell, and their families—for their love, support, and encouragement, even when they don't understand what I'm doing. My publishers, Henry B. Zimmer and Sue Blanchard, for their support, even when they weren't sure what I was doing. My editor, Gillian Steward, a friend and colleague, who sometimes knew what I was doing when I didn't. My friends, Gordon The Gardener, Bob Guilloux, 'Blind' John McCormick, and Will Burton, who listened to me talk about this book at length without telling me to shut up, and the musicians who encourage and enhance my other life. The people at Behavioral Health Consultants, the miracle workers who ensured I could sit in a chair long enough to finish this book, and Janet Jackson, who cheerily made sure the bills were paid. Gran, The Lady, The Little Lady, and The Other Woman.

The people who, wherever I travel, tell me stories, listen to mine, and in some way make me feel a little smarter after our conversations, specifically, IN CALGARY: Isaac Apt, Smithbilt Hats; Lynda Bockler, Underwear Mills; Linda Gardiner; Gerry Gribben, Gribben and Associates Management Consultants Ltd.; Mike Heffring, Stratix Research and Environics West; Paul and Bev Hughes, Mark Personnel Services Inc.; Hal Joffe, Barrister and Solicitor; Len LeSchack and Pam Vipond, Aquamarine Energy Exploration Ltd.; Kerry Sully, Ranchmen's Resources Ltd.; Chris Thomas, photographer; Darlene Murphy, D.M. Enterprises; Woody Rae, my partner in Straight Talk Communications Ltd.; George Steber, Spirit West Ltd.; Stan Stricker, Stratabound Minerals Corp.; Laszlo Uhrik, my partner in The Cowboy and The Continental Productions Ltd.; John and Lech Wojakowski, The Roasterie; the faculty, staff and students of the Professional

Writing Program at Mt. Royal College, who sometimes keep me on my toes about business. IN LONGVIEW, ALBERTA: Tom and Rosemarie Bews, their sons T.J., Guy, Dusty and Peter, Big Loop Cattle Co., and High Country Fishing Trips. IN TORONTO: Mark and Gerry Fine, AIRMAGIC Pyrotechnics and Special Effects; Dr. Barbara Moses, BBM Human Resources Consultants; Rene Schoepflin, Rene Schoepflin & Associates Inc.; Joan Hill, Core Consulting Inc.; Ted Mallett, senior economist, Canadian Federation of Independent Business. IN WINNIPEG/ VANCOUVER: Susan Jarema, Heather Worosz, As You Like; Bonnie Willimott, human resources counsellor. IN SUMMERSIDE, PEI: Jeannette Arsenault and Don Maxfield, Cavendish Figurines Ltd. IN SAN RAFAEL, CALIFORNIA: Mike Rausch. IN VANCOUVER/LOS ANGELES/THE AIR: Geoff Palmer, pilot extraordinaire. IN BOZEMAN, MONTANA: Dr. Ray Rasker, The Wilderness Society.

Contents

HUSTLING
FOR A
BUCK

THE ADVENTURE OF LIVING
SELF-EMPLOYED

CHAPTER ONE

The Adventure Begins

1995, September

Mugginess like a hot, damp cloak greeted Kevin Short when he arrived in Toronto. Even before he was off the plane and in the inadequately air-conditioned concourse of Terminal One at Pearson International Airport, his shirt was sticking to his back.

The noise, the closeness of the crowd, the heat…they pounded at him as he came down the escalator into the arrivals lounge and loaded a baggage cart with his computer and jacket. He pulled his tie loose as he nudged the cart towards the carousel.

Now we wait, he sighed, feeling more tired in spirit than in body. It had been a long three days getting back from Moscow, what with the meetings in Ottawa, hot, boring gabfests crushed under the weight of bureaucratic thinking and the awful, non-committal language of officialdom. Ah, whatever, he thought wryly, no sense in complaining. No one here cares if I'm in a foul mood; the other travellers probably feel the same way, as must those people who drove at a crawl through overheated traffic to meet them.

Kevin was content to find a cabbie to deliver him to his hotel alive. He could take another, later, to the conference.

The conference… He touched his jacket, where he had tucked his opening night speech. Tonight. Standing-room only, he had heard in the last message. He liked that. People voting with their wallets. Most of the people he and his colleagues from business and academia had taught over the last five years about being in business for themselves were coming. For a boost? New information? He shrugged. Who cared as long as they believed the conference was of value in their lives and businesses, and their expectations were met. That was enough. He smiled. Their continued participation was extra validation and reinforcement that what he and his colleagues did and believed in works, and was being received positively by the people it was directed to. It added a nice extra glow to success.

Again he touched the pocket with the speech. It's ready. All I need is a nap, then I'll be my bright and cheery self, ready to take on the world, he thought. Now, if I think cool, and focus on taking a cool shower, soaping away the miles and—

"You know, my kid brother never could keep his tie done up," a voice boomed behind him.

"Foolish things, anyway," Kevin said turning to greet his brother.

Kieron Short was 47, taller, wiry, with thinning dirty blonde hair, where his brother, two years his junior, was thin, with a mop of brown hair he wore parted in the centre and just brushing his collar. Kevin's next comment evaporated at sight of his brother's companions, four people he enjoyed seeing more than most other people he knew, but whom he didn't see enough, because their lives and businesses kept them spread all over the country, and the world.

Mac Sutherland…Kevin couldn't help but think of him as 'Big Mac', but he was a large man. Mac had picked up the nickname in the army, and it reappeared when he became a small-town cop. That had been long ago, and Kevin respected age and wisdom. Besides, Mac had command presence, important in someone who had built the third-largest, fastest-growing, national private security company. No, Kevin would never call Mac, who was about 56, 57, Big Mac.

John Tan looked as fit and cheeky and young as ever. Of course 45 looking back on 29 always has that perspective, no matter how fit the 45 believes himself to be. Kevin chuckled at the age image, recalling how John had once worried that his age, perfect for success in the youth-mad North American culture, would work against him in doing business in China, where age and seasoning are venerated. John had found a way to turn that cultural impediment into a profitable asset.

Susan Manyfingers looked too cool for this weather and this place, especially for someone who lived in Calgary and thrived on dry weather the way cactus does. All the travelling she was doing seemed to agree with her, because she looked much more poised than most 32-year-olds. Of course, she was doing business with art dealers and brokers the world over, some of whom paraded their arrogance and snobbery under the guise of elegance. Poise was a business asset she had cultivated to great advantage in dealing with the 'cultchuh vultchuhs'.

The real shock, and a pleasant one at that, was Brenda Bashford. She had shed those extra pounds that still clung to her when they last met, about—a year ago, he marvelled—on her thirty-sixth birthday, when he and Danielle stopped in Vancouver, on their way home from Los Angeles. Losing the weight wasn't such a remarkable feat, people do it all the time, but it was notable in that Brenda did it while operating (and owning) one of Vancouver's most successful niche-market upscale restaurants.

"Now what are you people doing here?" he asked with an affectionate smile for all. He had taught many people about business in the five years The Oswego Program had been operating, but he felt a deeper bond with and fondness for the people he had taught in its first year. "You ought to be powdering your noses, or whatever you feel you have to do to be ready to speak at the conference. You're among our star attractions."

"We wanted to surprise you, brother," Kieron said, laughing. "We thought you might be so jet lagged it would take all five of us to carry you and Danielle out to the limo." He looked around. "Where is Danielle?"

"Limo?" Kevin asked.

Kieron shrugged. "Actually it's the college passenger van. Budget restraints. Where's Danielle?"

"She went on to Peterborough, to pick up Rachel, and see her parents," Kevin said. "She's already heard my speech, two or three versions of it, and she was anxious to see Rachel—it's been a long summer without her. Danielle wanted to get her right away and bring her here to catch some of the conference. She'll be here Sunday to do her bit. Don't worry."

Kieron pointed to himself. "Me worried?" He shook his head. "I've missed her as much as I missed you. I was looking forward to seeing her, too." He smiled and cocked his head. "Well, then, once we've collected your bags, your transport awaits you."

"I can just see you showing up in a limo," Kevin chuckled.

"Yes, but I know how much you dislike anything that smacks of extravagance, brother," Kieron sighed. "Can't treat you to anything."

"Damned right," Kevin growled. "If you don't need it, don't waste money on it!"

"No, please, not again," Brenda begged. "I'm just starting to enjoy managing the money it takes to start and run a restaurant. I still wake up in a cold panic, repeating your peeves." She struck a lecturish pose, held out both hands to her audience and said, in a passable imitation of Kevin, "Now government has to stop trying to act like business should, and business has to stop acting like governments should, and..."

"Whoa, whoa, I'm glad to be back," Kevin said soberly, his hands high. "And I love this place. No matter how weird things get here, I remind myself that in Moscow, and everywhere I went in Russia, I was escorted everywhere by a big guy named Yevgenyi, who had a conspicuous bulge under his jacket, and whose job was to keep me from being kidnapped and held for ransom."

"That's why I'm not looking at Russia as a market for quite a while," Susan said. "What's the use of doing business if you can't enjoy yourself, and get out of it alive?"

"Exactly, just what I said to Kieron when he asked me what I thought of The Oswego Program when it was starting up," Kevin grinned.

. . . .

1990, June: *Ontario Cottage Country*

"So, what do you think of the course outline?" Kieron Short asked his brother.

"A micro-business incubator..." Kevin rolled the words over his tongue. "A place to nurture a business attitude." He mulled that one a moment before shaking his head. "I think you'll short-change your clients," he said.

"Clients...?"

"Yeah, clients. Think of your students as clients. You're the service provider, but you're still thinking like the principal of a prestigious technical college. You have to balance what the clients want and need with what you want to do, and what you think they need, so they come away from this experience prepared to face being

4

in business without panicking. They're consumers paying for the service," Kevin said. "Deliver."

"Well, them and the taxpayer," Kieron replied.

"Well, then, treat the taxpayers like clients, too, and give them their value added for backing you—successes," Kevin said. "Organize for success in a business context, see success stories as your profit, and present them to others as learning models."

"That's what we want to, uh, need to do," Kieron insisted.

"Then don't let the program become academic, which this design is," Kevin said, pointing at the report. "If you want to nurture the entrepreneurial spirit in people, get a mix of academics, bureaucrats and retired businesspeople to teach the program, but have someone with a vision of business, someone who does business, and thinks about it, run the show, like a business. Value added."

"Who then?" Kieron asked.

"Well," Kevin shifted uncomfortably on the lounge and sipped his drink. "Real businesspeople, not the bureaucrats who run big businesses, but people who have actually started and run micro- or small businesses, and grew them to between $25 million and $100 million—$125 million tops—cash flow annually."

"Small pool to choose from, there," Kieron said.

"I'll give you some names. Some good people are available because of the consolidation rage," Kevin said. "If one of them goes for your idea, you'll get good service in running a program for people who haven't conducted business and think it's a big, risky mystery."

"We're committed to helping people change that attitude," Kieron said. "To...helping them learn, before going into business, something of what business is about."

Kevin nodded in agreement, and sympathy, for Kieron's position. Kieron had been away from hands-on business since he left his law practice, though even as a partner in a legal practice, he had been buffered from business management by professional managers. As principal of Oswego College, he tried to run the place as much like a business as he could, but there were too many years of practice, too many ties to too many procedures that made the task as challenging as trying to turn the Queen Elizabeth II in the Houston Ship Channel.

"Academics can teach business theory, but if they haven't been in business for themselves, it's only theory," Kevin continued.

"Theory has to be taught in tandem with practical knowledge, which you can only get from experienced businesspeople. They might not know the theories, but they will know what business is, and does. And experience has to be the primary teacher if your incubator is to be effective, or you're just setting people up with false expectations that could cause as much trouble for them as blind ignorance."

"Okay, you're hired," Kieron grinned.

"Hired?" Kevin almost choked on his drink. "Me? You have to be out of your head!"

"No, I'm not. Dad and I know just how much wealth you created from virtually nothing with A Chip Off The Old Block," Kieron smiled.

"You guys backed the start-up," Kevin shrugged.

"But you were the visionary who built the business," Kieron said. "Given the wealth you created for me, my kids will never have to worry for their futures."

"Spend it on yourself," Kevin muttered. "Let them earn their way, like we did." He coughed. "And don't make the mistake of believing your press clippings. People lose fortunes when they let their egos get in the way of business."

"I know," Kieron laughed. "But you *are* one of the success stories of the decade. You turned an $80,000 investment in one computer shop into a multi-million-dollar discount computer store chain in nine years."

"Nine years is a lot of time," Kevin shrugged. "And I didn't set out to make a fortune. I just saw a challenging opportunity. I was lucky."

"And maybe in the right place at the right time, and all those other cliches about life, business and fortune, but that's immaterial," Kieron said. "To my mind, you're the best one to tell me what's right and wrong with the program design, to help me fix it, and to teach part of the program. Besides, you aren't exactly busy."

They both looked over the railing on the deck to the lake at the end of the lot and grinned. What had started as a single computer store, where Kevin could be his own boss and make a living in peace, had turned into six years of whirlwind growth and a nationwide chain of 45 stores. Kevin had, however, wanted out of A Chip Off The Old Block, ever since the day the year before when he realized he wasn't creating anything new with each store opening, but only recreating something he had done before. The adventure was gone; he wasn't having fun any more. He had recognized his business strength was nurturing ideas, not running them once they were reality, and he knew he had to get out, otherwise neither he nor the business would prosper past that point. Then Elmag, the electronics conglomerate, had approached him a third time to buy the company, and made an outrageously generous offer.

Kevin didn't believe the company was worth what Elmag offered, but Elmag management thought the price was still cheaper than the cost to create a new discount chain and fight a price war no one could win. He told his three partners, his wife, father and brother, it was time to sell, take the cash and Elmag stock packages, consolidate as much as possible, then discreetly sell off the Elmag stock as soon as possible. He had little faith in a company management eager to pay more for something than it was realistically worth, just to avoid having to get into competition.

The sale had closed three weeks before, and Kevin had defied convention by declining a contract to stay on as president. If Elmag wanted to grow to 80 stores, let someone else expand the empire. So, A Chip had a new president, though Kevin had agreed to a three-year consulting contract. He was also bound by a five-year, non-competition agreement for which Elmag had paid a premium on the purchase price of his shares. If they had only known how bored he had been with board meetings, Elmag's bosses could have saved a bundle. So there he sat, unwinding, taking the sun, and sipping a Pina Colada on the balcony of his and Danielle's Pine Lake cottage, only a two-hour drive from Toronto, watching his wife of 15 years paint, and their six-year-old daughter swim.

"If you really want the incubator to work, give them intensity in the program," Kevin suggested. "Make the school reality close to the business reality they'll be facing. Make them test their tolerance for risk. Make them understand they're in business to make money, that their fundamental task is doing business...that they're always in a transaction of some sort."

"So, just for argument's sake, Kevin, tell me what you'd do with this." Kieron hefted the binder with the course outline.

"Surgery. Cut half the academic courses and run them Tuesday to Thursday mornings, and only as forums for lectures and other instruction about practical matters. Save the afternoons for skills development labs like using computers, negotiation simulations, sales scenarios, that sort of thing, taught by experienced people. It's as close as they'll get to real business as long as they're in school."

Kieron scrawled notes in the binder.

"Make the lectures and labs in the first two weeks familiarization sessions, round-robin presentations by the instructors on management issues, so everyone can get a feel for each other. Then make the students pitch themselves as proteges to the instructors in the third week, each instructor to take on four or five students. From then on, we reserve Mondays and Fridays for mentoring sessions—"

"We," Kieron interrupted. "You said 'we'. You're in?"

Kevin looked at his brother in surprise. "Well, I guess I am intrigued by the idea. If you do it the way I suggest, I'd be so surprised I might be willing to try."

"Not try," Kieron shook his head slowly. "Commit! I want you for a year. You can work out your schedules with Elmag, but you're mine for a year, for a dollar."

"Hell, let's see if we can get Elmag to sponsor my role in your faculty on my consulting contract. They might like the publicity."

"So you're in?" Kieron demanded.

"There are only three months until the program begins. Can you make the changes?"

"It'll be a stretch, and I'll have to twist a few arms, hard..." Kieron thought a moment. "Yeah, I think I can do it," he assured him with a chuckle. "What's the point of being principal of the college if I can't shake things up now and then?"

"Whoa, Kieron, you're too political an animal to have just cooked this up," Kevin said suspiciously. "You like to win too much. I think you've already done your arm-twisting act and laid the groundwork for these kinds of, uh, changes."

Kieron smiled benignly. "Are you in?"

"Let me check with Danielle, and..."

CHAPTER TWO

Getting to the Art of the Matter

1995, September: *An Auditorium at Oswego College*

"...and understand I've known our keynote speaker for 45 years, ever since he began making a big noise, not as a businessman, or teacher, but as my newly arrived baby brother. So nothing he says surprises me," Kieron said from the lectern at the front of the auditorium. He was pleased. The conference was a box-office success. "However, he has come here straight from Moscow, where he was part of a study group assessing the feasibility of setting up an incubator such as ours in partnership with the Russian and Canadian governments. Perhaps he'll have something to say that *will* surprise me. Ladies and gentlemen, Kevin Short."

Kevin disliked the formula for public speaking: Tell an amusing story, break the ice, get the auidence's attention, get on with the speech. The problems with the formula, he believed, after having been exposed to it all too often, are that it's predictable, most people don't know how to tell a joke, and, more often than not, the joke or story has no bearing on the talk and just confuses the listener. Well, tonight he was going to go against his biases, because he had a story to tell.

"When my paternal grandfather came to Canada early in this century, he came from a part of Hungary where the names were long and difficult for English speakers to pronounce," he began. "The official who processed his entry into the country looked at the papers and said, 'This won't do at all. Too complicated. We have to change it.'

"Grandpa just shrugged and replied, 'You are the government man. You can do whatever you want. But please, when you give me my new name, make it short.'

"So the government man made our family name Short."

The audience laughed, and Kevin was thankful for that as he

paused and prepared himself for the next part of his speech—the kicker. He took a breath and launched into it: "Now I tell you this story, because, as keynote speaker, I'm supposed to set the tone for this conference. And the tone I want to set is this: Those of us who seek to become independent businesspeople, to create something for ourselves, our children, our colleagues, are like that 'government man'. All of us...each of us has the power to do whatever he or she wants to do, *if we can unleash that power.*

"We *can* unleash that power. We must take the brakes off our imaginations, our souls and our energies. We must be open to constant change, and we must re-educate ourselves, and grow, not all at once, but continually. And we must do it, starting now, one day at a time, every day, for the rest of our lives..."

....

1995, The Conference: *Kieron*

I shudder to think what would happen if Kevin ever went into politics, Kieron thought as he listened to his younger brother's speech. When he gets going on something he believes in, he's like a steamroller. Lord knows, he would make some changes, though his way of doing it would be to relocate the nation's capital out in the middle of the Prairies and start over from scratch.

It's better that he does what he's doing now, some teaching, some consulting, and managing his investments. He has a saying for it—he loves good sayings, creates or collects them all the time— *We can't change the world. We can only change ourselves. Then the world changes.* He loves words and ideas so much, he never invests in any company where his brains aren't welcome. So now he owns pieces of a number of interesting little companies with big futures, run by people with big ideas who sit in council with him, and seek his counsel. What a combination!

I wish we'd had more time to talk about his thoughts on the Russia project, but that can wait until after the conference. Right now, we have to carry through and serve up a quality weekend to our clients, as Kevin calls them. The 200 people we've put through our incubator program, who are back for a boost, the 200 people who want to take the program and hope this will give them an edge to get in, the 100 observers from governments, business and other institutions who all talk about promoting business development—they're all in for an interesting weekend.

Two hundred graduates. We've come a long way from the pilot project of the first 20 in '90. I guess this is my version of A Chip Off The Old Block.

. . . .

1990, September: *A Lecture Theatre, Oswego College, Toronto*

Kevin Short shuffled his papers and looked nervously at the 20 students and eight faculty members waiting for Kieron to finish the introductions and hear what he had to say. The butterflies in his stomach had been flying in formation when he came in, but now they were having dogfights. He had taken up Kieron's challenge, and now it was time to act, and teach. Whoops, that word teach sent those butterflies at each other again with renewed vigor.

He got up, placed his notes on the lectern and paced slowly before the chalk boards as he spoke.

"We can do anything in life. *You can do anything in life,*" he said slowly, randomly making eye contact with people in the room as he spoke. "But before any of us can do anything, we must establish for ourselves a foundation, a clear vision of the world in which we operate. We must base that vision, that world-view, on a reality, but we walk on shifting sands when we speak about reality, because each of us has a different set of experiences and values through which we filter what we see around us. What results is our individual realities. We just have to recognize them, honor them, work with them."

Kevin stopped and pointed to a large man with silver-streaked hair.

"Your name, sir?"

"Mac Sutherland. Call me Mac."

"Please, Mac, give us a thumbnail autobiography."

"My full name is Mackenzie Sutherland. I'm 52, and I was born in Winnipeg. I was 18 when I joined the army in 1956. I was a military policeman for 15 years, then a civilian cop in Whitby,

11

Ontario for almost five years before joining the security department of the Provincial Bank of Canada, where I worked for 12 years, before becoming chief of security, which I've been for three years."

"What schooling did you have, and what rank did you hold when you left the Forces, Mac?"

"I was commissioned from the ranks and was a Captain when I retired. I took a university degree in criminology by night school and correspondence while in the Forces, and I've taken criminal fraud courses organized by the Royal Canadian Mounted Police, the U.S. Federal Bureau of Investigation, and U.S. Secret Service."

"So you specialized in criminal fraud?"

The class and visitors laughed. Kevin laughed with them.

"Only as a hobby," Mac said with a sly grin, triggering more laughter, and surprising Kevin. The older man had seemed too serious to joke around. "General police work is what I did most, but fraud, especially credit card scams and counterfeiting, just fascinated me. I took the courses, established a network of friendly professional contacts, and became known as a bit of an expert on credit card fraud."

"And that's how you came to work for the bank?"

"Yes, sir."

"Please, call me Kevin, Mac. Now, why are you here?"

"The bank redefined the structure of my department, which changed my job," Mac said. "It makes my job an administrative one, and I'm not an administrator, not the way they want me to be. My choices were keep my job and become a bureaucrat, stay and not adjust, with the inevitable consequence of being purged some other way, or leave."

"And you resigned."

"Well, not before I negotiated a nice severance package, which, with the help of a couple of shrewd financial planners, I invested carefully," Mac said. "The bank also has a program to pay my full salary for up to two years, as long as I'm looking for new work, or preparing to set myself up in my own business."

"From a bank?" Kevin chuckled.

Mac shrugged. "They put it in my job description and agreement, and we all signed it."

"Wonder of wonders," Kevin said as he shook his head slowly in admiration of Mac's initiative in defining and using an opportunity to his advantage. "Hmmm. So you have the luxury of time to learn...what? What do you expect to learn here?"

"Well, I want to set up a private security firm, but I want to do it right." He hesitated and looked around the room, then shrugged. "I don't know if you want me to talk about it, but, well, the numbers on success rates for first-time business start-ups..."

"Oh, please, be my guest," Kevin laughed. "This is the part I was dreading most—first the bad news, etcetera—so *you* be the bad guy in the group."

"The people in the commercial banking division at the bank showed me a bunch of studies that weren't encouraging...that at least 50 per cent and as much as 85 per cent of start-ups will fail within the first five years."

"The large statistical range aside, did they tell you *why* the failure rate is so high?" Kevin asked.

Mac nodded. "Inadequate management skills."

"Which means...what?" Kevin asked.

"Their administration skills weren't strong?" Mac offered.

"Likely, but having weak administrative skills, or lacking them altogether, still isn't the quick business killer," Kevin said. "Tell me, anyone, what are we in business to do?"

No one answered.

"Come on," Kevin prompted. "The only stupid question is the one left unasked; the only stupid answer is the one unvoiced and left unchallenged." He looked around hopefully. "No takers? Okay, here goes. We're all hustling for a buck. *We are in business to profit from buying and selling things.* Got that?"

He looked at the people in the class, making eye contact with as many as he could.

"Please, work with me," he said. "I need reinforcement. Nod for yes. Shake your heads for no."

They laughed as they nodded.

"Thank you," Kevin sighed. "Now understand that seeking profit is good, but being greedy without purpose makes us destructive of ourselves, the people around us and the environment. Keep in mind the stock-market aphorism: *Bulls make money. Bears make money. Pigs get slaughtered.* Got that?"

There was more laughter as people's heads bobbed up and down.

"Understand that everything we do besides creating and trading is, or should be, administration in support of those tasks, *to ensure we do not spend more than we earn*," Kevin said. "Any diversion from that relationship will create a bureaucratic mess that chokes you in paperwork."

"Well, I'm here to learn how to manage effectively, and have a better chance at success, without getting choked up in expensive management," Mac said. "I have a finite amount of start-up money and reserves, I'm in my fifties, with one more child left to put through university. I don't want to blow my chances because I don't know what I'm doing."

"Your world-view is cautious and conservative, but at least focused on moving forward."

Mac nodded. "I think it's the best strategy for my circumstances."

"Reasonable. Tell me—and this isn't to embarrass anyone— but does anyone here feel any desperate need to go into business *immediately?* You know, like you have to do it tomorrow, or you're doomed, and this program suddenly seems like a waste of time?"

A woman at the back of the room raised her hand. "I'm just feeling mixed up about the whole thing."

"And you are?"

"Brenda Bashford."

"Brenda?" he asked and looked to see if she would object to his using her first name. She didn't stop him. "What do you think is the problem, Brenda?"

"I think it's money and time," she said. "I mean we're booked in here for classes to mid-April. That's eight months before I can even begin thinking about starting a business."

"Good point. Ultimately, no matter what we do, whether we offer goods or services, those *things* we are actually selling are bits of our time, and we want to make those minutes earn the most we can," Kevin said. "I think of it this way: *Life is short. Dead is a long time. Make the most of life.*" He looked at Brenda, his eyes almost boring into her. "So why are you here?"

"Because I'm like Mac, in a way," she said. "I'm a Certified General Accountant, but I quit working four years ago when I got pregnant. I just got divorced, I have custody of my three-year-old son, and I have a small stake from the sale of our house. I'm not sure how long I can count on Danny's father to pay child support. So I want to go back to work, but I'm not sure I want to work for other people, or even as an accountant."

"I see," Kevin said. "Understand that no consultant, government or private business development advisor, accountant, or lawyer would ever advise you to rush into business. Not unless you're in a hurry to lose a lot of money," he shrugged.

"I would even have been one of those accountants," Brenda said. "But it's different on the receiving end of the advice. Eight months! It seems so long."

"It could be," Kevin agreed. "But I understand that a week looks like an eternity when you have to face getting control of a business that's more like a runaway train," Kevin said. He paused for a moment to let that idea register. "Why don't you make your studies work double for you? Get your thinking sorted out while you learn. Do you have any idea of what you want to do?"

"No, not really," she said. "I was thinking of a store of some kind."

"Do you have experience in retailing?" Kevin asked.

"No," she said.

"Well, now you can start to focus. Sort yourself out," Kevin said gently. "This is as good a place as any to do it, and it's cheaper than losing a bundle on a business project you take on that goes sour because you didn't prepare yourself." He turned his attention to the entire class. "Look, there are many resources we can call on for help, but we have to stretch our imaginations to do that, if we want to create and build a business." He shrugged. "I know it's little comfort to those of you on limited resources. But what are the options? Give up? I don't see that as a realistic choice. I operate on the principle that *if there's something you need, but don't have, you haven't asked for it. Ask for it, and you'll find a way to get it."*

"Easy for you to say. You have it made," another female voice called out. "I know people who have been unemployed for 18 months and want to work," the woman continued. "They've sent out hundreds of resumes, and sold their houses. They see their money running out. They're desperate."

"Then they haven't accepted that the world isn't what they expected it to be, and it's time to reinvent their lives and ideas about work, about values," Kevin replied. "They have to understand booms always go bust—"

He nodded emphatically as some of his listeners responded with exaggerated, theatrical groans.

"Yes! I'm sorry to say: *The party always ends.* And I was as saddened to learn that as you," he said. "I learned it in Calgary, where I lived for two years in the '70s, and which I visited every 10 weeks or so when I ran A Chip. They have a boom or a bust there about every 15 minutes, it seems," he said wryly. "Hearing about and watching the experiences of my friends and contacts there, and in other places outside Toronto, made me learn to continually examine life and what happens in our world. That's why I suggest you construct for yourself a world-view that will give a context to how you do business and lead your life."

He walked back to the blackboard and wrote 1880 on one panel, 1975 on another, and 1990 on a third. He drew a large circle around the 1880.

"In the research I've done, formal and conversational, 1880 is acknowledged as the year the first drops of crude oil lubricated, and began to supply energy for industry. It was the beginning of the mass economy phase of the industrial revolution."

He wrote 90% and 10% under the 1880.

"At that time, nine out of 10 people who worked were small business operators—shopkeepers, shoemakers, seamstresses, repair-men, blacksmiths, farmers," Kevin said as he wrote the occupations on the board. "Ninety per cent were self employed."

He moved to the 1975 panel, and drew a tombstone around the date.

"This is the year the mass economy died," he said. "Three years after the 1972 oil shock, governments the world over were subsidizing the price of oil through tax breaks or direct injections of cash that bankrupted their treasuries, then drove them into deficit financing. All this to keep their industries, or populations supplied with cheap energy. But it was a wasted effort, because the costs of finding and transporting oil to market began to escalate, and have steadily eroded the cost-benefit of oil as a cheap energy source."

"So what? I can still fill my car for between 49 and 55 cents a litre. It's manageable," someone called to Kevin.

"Only because big OPEC oil producers like Saudi Arabia are dumping all the oil they can produce to keep the cash flowing in," Kevin said. "Gas is cheap, because there are oil gluts on the world market. The problem is, the oil they're pumping and selling cheaply now is selling for less, much less, than what it costs to replace with new reserves of oil, or oil available from new wells."

"And we, the consumers, are getting a price break," someone else called out. "I remember when prices were even higher."

"And they'll go higher again, unless the costs of finding and exploiting new reserves decline. So translate that into what it costs to operate a factory, and what it's like to plan, when your energy costs can shift by as much as 25 per cent two or three times a year, without warning," Kevin suggested. "You, sir," Kevin pointed to the man who talked about filling his tank. "Please, stand up. Your name?"

"Paul Burnham."

"Okay, Paul, say you're a factory owner. Your cheapest fixed cost, energy, becomes a high and fluctuating cost. It makes you uncompetitive. What do you do?"

Burnham shrugged. "Why, I look for where I can cut other costs."

"And what do you find?"

"Uh, I'm not sure," he said uncomfortably.

"Anyone?"

"Your employee costs," Brenda Bashford said. "You can control them by adjusting the size of workforce, the wages you pay them, benefits, and the productivity you require."

"Exactly! This is why *you all* need to learn to construct and read balance sheets and profit and loss statements. Even non-financial people must learn to see what accountants and Big Business operators see, and how they think. That's why so many of you are looking for jobs, or are being forced to create jobs or businesses for yourselves," Kevin said. "These guys don't see *people,* they see *costs,* and these costs are alternatively fixed, fluctuating, manageable, or negotiable."

He broke off what he was saying to write the four words on the board, underline them each twice, then drop the chalk on the ledge. Turning back to the group, he rapped the board.

"You can't negotiate oil prices, and they change with the weekly fixes in the per barrel price. So you can't easily project energy costs," he said. "For that matter, you can't negotiate interest rates either, unless you're so big it's in a lender's interests to give you a deal just to get your business. You can also get a break, maybe, on materials, but your single biggest manageable cost is people."

"And they're cheaper to employ in Mexico and Malaysia, or Thailand," Brenda said. "So manufacturing jobs leave."

"You've got it! *Capital goes where it can get the best return on its deployment,*" Kevin said as he moved to the third blackboard panel where he wrote 10% and 90% under 1990, which he circled. "Which leaves us here, where, if we had full employment, 10 per cent would be self employed and 90 per cent would be job holders."

He waited for the information to sink in. "However, what's really happening is the ratio is shifting, and has been for a decade, but most dramatically in the last three years," he said. "For whatever reasons people do it, they have been starting their own businesses at an accelerating rate since 1979, while total jobs available have been declining."

He looked at his audience, all 29 of them sitting there, apparently absorbed. "Are you following me?" he interrupted himself.

Everyone nodded.

"Okay," he called out and went on. "So, as I said, the ratio is changing again. To what? I don't know, but some people say we could see 70, even 80 per cent self employment by 2010, and *in work and businesses we don't even think of as work or businesses today.*"

"So those people busily seeking jobs, are part of a larger pool of people chasing a smaller...and shrinking pool of jobs," Brenda offered.

"Yes," Kevin sighed. "And the challenge is to change more than 40 years of thinking and social processes. Since 1945, people have been taught that if they fitted in, played by the rules, and kept their noses clean, there would be a job for each for life. And the promise hasn't been kept."

"Amen to that," a man called from the back of the room. He stood up. "My name's Stan, Stan Everett. I'm 36, and I love retail merchandising. I gave 12 years of loyal service to The Grange stores. Their profit margins weren't right, so they brought in a high-priced consultant and a few weeks later, a whole floor of buyers was out the door, into the hands of outplacement people...their 'thank you'."

"So are you going to keep complaining about it?" Kevin asked.

"I'm here, because I have no time to waste on what's been," Everett said. "As far as I'm concerned, the best revenge is success."

"So...what? You expect to learn some magical quick-fix secret to success here?" Kevin demanded.

"If you have one, I'd like to hear it," Everett replied. "And if you do, I'd like to know how you stayed out of prison."

"That's a piece of wisdom you would all do well to remember," Kevin said when the laughter died out. "The only ways I know to get rich quick will eventually get you a trek to the poorhouse, an extended holiday at one of Her Majesty's re-education resorts for wayward boys and girls, or both."

The laughter sounded a little nervous this time.

"But you aren't necessarily doomed to doing hard time on Planet Earth, struggling to make ends meet," Kevin quickly reassured them. "Being in business can be quite an exciting and lucrative adventure. It's even better when what you do is fun, and contributes to the quality of your life. So start thinking that if a difficulty, such as divorce, layoff or some other misfortune got you here, it wasn't the end of something, but a learning experience, and the beginning of a new opportunity."

He searched slowly for an eraser and more chalk so this idea could sink in.

"The first thing we need to do is recognize that the nature of work is changing, and we need to change a whole bunch of ideas and stereotypes we hold as true," Kevin said. "The key here is that the work we did exclusively for others for a salary was only a *job*. Work we do, or the goods we provide for a variety of people we recruit as our clients, for fees, or payment for goods, from which we seek personal profit, is our *business*," Kevin said as he wrote furiously on the board. "And you must understand that business is the carrying on of transactions among *individuals*, even if they represent companies. Which means—" He moved to a clean board and wrote in large letters, "—business isn't exclusively what goes on between people in office parks, or towers, in stores or malls. It is the exchange of goods or services between or among individuals to meet the need of one for that good or service, and the need of another for cash or some other good or service of equal or greater value."

"By that definition, anything can be considered a business," Brenda objected.

"Say it again, many times, until you believe it, Brenda, and you're halfway to success. One of my mottos is," and he wrote on the last clean board:

LOOK AT LIFE LIKE A BUSINESSPERSON
Define What Opportunity Means To You, So You Can Recognize It
When You See It
THINK LIKE A BUSINESSPERSON
Always Keep Your Eyes Open For Opportunity
ACT LIKE A BUSINESSPERSON
Always Be Prepared To Exploit What You See As Opportunity
STUDY THE WORLD LIKE A BUSINESSPERSON
Always Keep Your Mind Open To New Ideas, New Information
And New Wisdom
CONDUCT BUSINESS IN AN ETHICAL MANNER
Never Treat People In A Way You Would Not Tolerate Being
Treated Yourself. Let Honesty, Integrity, Courtesy And Loyalty
Be Your Guides. Always Deliver What You Promise, And Never
Promise What You Can't Deliver
WITH ENOUGH PRACTICE, YOU'LL BE A BUSINESSPERSON

Kevin stepped back from his handiwork and reread it, then dropped the chalk on the ledge.

"Let's break for coffee, and reconvene here in 20 minutes," he said as he brushed his hands together to wipe off the chalk dust.

. . . .

"As I said, I know people in Calgary, where the boom died much earlier than here in Toronto," Kevin began when everyone was seated again. "Three years ago, I was visiting our Calgary managers, and accompanied one of our people to install a computer system in a donut shop..."

The franchise owner, Mike Tesch, had been an exploration geologist who lost his job in the second round of oil company restructurings in 1985. After 18 frustrating months of looking for a new job in the oil industry, he decided to create his own job, but, because he had little experience in business, and, because of his job loss, Tesch was risk shy, so he decided to buy a franchise. He needed something inexpensive, recession-proof, that sold a product, so he wouldn't again be vulnerable to demand, or lack of it, for his skills or training.

The most recession-proof business around appeared to be a fast-food franchise, and a donut shop with its limited product line was the quickest to learn to operate. So, after researching the opportunities, Tesch decided to buy a donut franchise. He used a portion of his severance package, and borrowed from members of his family to raise the money to buy and operate the shop. The franchise made him a comfortable living his first year, turned a modest profit, and positioned him to start repaying the family members who backed his purchase.

"So should we all go out and buy franchises?" a woman demanded. "Is that the key to the future?"

"Not necessarily, but a business is a business," Kevin responded. "As long as it covers its costs, pays you a decent living wage, and turns a profit, do you care what the business is?"

"But what about fun and challenge?" the woman demanded. "I moved here from Calgary to take this program. I know Mike Tesch, even go for coffee at his shop when I'm in Calgary—"

"Could you identify yourself before you go on?" Kevin asked.

The woman stood up. "I'm Susan Manyfingers. I'm 28, a Blood Indian from the Lethbridge, Alberta, area. I have a fine arts degree from the University of Western Ontario—"

"Ah, my alma mater, too," Kevin offered.

"—and, when I worked on *The Spirit Sings,* an exhibit of Indian artifacts held during the Calgary Winter Olympics, I saw all these tourists going crazy to buy Indian art, and raving about how hard it is to get at home. So I want to start a business marketing and exporting contemporary Native Canadian art to foreign markets. This way, I can help young Native artists get established."

"Sounds interesting. Thank you, Susan. You were saying about Mike..."

"He's financially secure now. I spoke with him a few weeks ago. He's prospering, crazy in love with a woman he knew from his old company, and they're getting married next year."

"I hear a 'but' coming, Susan."

She nodded. "But he has moments when he isn't sure he's better off," Susan said. "He misses not using his brain, you know...for what he was trained to do." She sat down.

"But Susan, we are who we are, long before we're identified by what we studied, or do for a living," Kevin said. "I was trained as an engineer, but it doesn't bother me that I haven't built any bridges, or big mechanical projects."

"No, but you built an impressive merchandising empire," someone shouted. "That beats a bridge any time."

Kevin laughed with everyone else. "Who said that?"

"John Tan, University of Toronto, Engineering, '89," a young Asian man said in unaccented English. "And I'm not sure I want to build bridges either. I just like systems. I'm looking at setting up a consultancy with one of my relatives in Hong Kong, to act as intermediaries...you know, a bridge between China and North American industry."

"John, at first thought, that's a brilliant idea," Kevin said. He crossed his arms and tapped his chin as he thought a moment. "As for A Chip Off The Old Block becoming the success it is, well, I have to tell you it happened more by accident than design, at least the empire part of it." He began to pace again. "I was frustrated working for Consolidated Computer Corp. They were building these huge expensive mainframe systems, and making each new generation incompatible with the previous generation..."

Kevin shook his head, almost in wonder, as he recalled his days selling and installing systems for Three C, as it was called, after he left university in 1974 with his engineering degree. His clients were always muttering about how they wished they could have something like a mainframe at everyone's desk. The two years he spent in Calgary, doing his time getting his ticket punched before moving on to Vancouver, then upstairs in the Three C marketing department in Toronto, were quite educational.

In Calgary, he had watched the oil industry's massive appetite for data processing eat up computer power faster than he could install the systems. It was like feeding an elephant. As soon as a job was done and the clean-up completed, he had to start all over again.

Then he did an installation at one of the newspapers in town and saw how production could be streamlined if each reporter had a terminal feeding directly to the composing room, and, suddenly, he had his world-view. He saw how individual, stand-alone, desktop computers were going to change the world, and his role in that would be as the person who provided the best machines available, at the most reasonable prices.

"It took me two more years of fruitlessly trying to get management to buy into the idea of creating and selling a desktop computer line before I got up the courage to start A Chip Off The Old Block," Kevin said. "By then, Apple was selling its first, primitive— by today's standards—home computers. Rumor had it IBM was coming out with a personal computer, and all sorts of smaller operators were either producing exotic and expensive introductory machines, or had products they would soon bring to market."

"So you went out, opened your first store at Yonge and Eglinton, and became an overnight success," John Tan said.

"I wish," Kevin laughed. "I learned overnight success is years in the making, John. Try this on for a week: planning the business; designing the store; finding suppliers; deciding on a product mix; raising money; finding the right location; getting the best banking services; opening a relationship with a banker; negotiating leases; getting licences, building permits, signage and advertising. Though it only took six months, setting up shop seemed to go on forever, but it was a new concept in '81—the consumer computer store. I learned *we must do what we have to, sometimes things we don't like to do, so we can do what we want to.*"

"Sure," Brenda said. "Easy for you to say. You don't have to work another day in your life."

"That's now, and I earned it, but I know of faster ways to commit suicide than living the life of the idle rich," Kevin shot back. "The first year A Chip Off The Old Block was operating, we had lean times. That was 1981–2, when personal computers were expensive toys, businesses were still stuck with mainframes and sceptical about the role of the then-available desktops, and my main competition was confusion on the consumer's part."

"Is that when you came up with the company slogan?" John asked. "Cobol, Fortran and English spoken here."

Kevin laughed. "Actually, what happened was an important piece of marketing information walked in my door one day, in the form of a writer who hated retyping her manuscripts. She had found she spent as much on typing services each year as it would cost to buy a computer, a printer, and word processing software..."

She had had a problem, though, Kevin recalled. She understood nothing about computers, and only wanted to learn as much as was necessary to make an informed decision. That's how she had bought a car; she figured she could buy a computer with the same level of information. However, whenever she talked with people in the new computer stores, some boob of a salesman would offend her with the 'Here, let me help you, little lady' approach, and bombard her with information couched in computer 'Newspeak' that overwhelmed her. All she wanted was someone to speak to her in no-nonsense, simple English, and help her to get her hands on that wonderful facility computers had of being able to move paragraphs around without having to retype a whole manuscript.

Kevin listened, and not only helped her, but learned from her how to listen to individual consumers and make them his paying clients by meeting their needs. She and most of the practical early users—and most since—wanted and needed simple, clear explanations on how to improve their productivity with computers. They would sell themselves on the purchase.

She just wanted to plug in the computer, turn it on, and get on with her work. So he got her a computer called a Kaypro II, what was then called a portable, though it weighed about 40 pounds. It was, however, simple to operate, compact, with a screen built into the case, and reliable. The best price he could give her on the computer and a printer was $3,200. He set up the computer and let it run in his store for three days, then spent a half hour showing her how to operate it when she came to pick it up. Two weeks later, he called her to see how she was getting along with her computer, and she was effusive in her professions of loyalty to him and his store.

She started sending her writer friends to see him, and he was surprised to find out there were so many different kinds of working writers in the country, let alone so many who could afford computers. He met public relations writers, technical writers, manual writers, advertising writers, book, script...the list went on. Some had corporate jobs and wanted a way of doing work at home. Some were freelance and worked at home all the time. Then Kevin did some research and found these people constituted a market he hadn't even anticipated. He contacted the four major national writers groups in the country, and offered volume discount packages to their members who bought through group plans.

"In 1983, I sold and shipped 200 systems to writers in Toronto, and all over the country," Kevin said. "I also negotiated volume discounts on my costs from suppliers, so the more I sold at the discounted price, the better my profit margin, and the better the deals I could offer."

"But you couldn't have depended on 200 computer sales alone," Brenda said.

"No, but those 200 computers paid the rent on the store that year," Kevin pointed out. "And by then consumers were better informed, not only about computers, but about us. 'Cobol, Fortran and English spoken here' was our motto, and our style, and people appreciated it. They brought us their business, because we spoke *with* them, not *at* them."

"So when did you become an overnight success?" John Tan demanded.

"The foundation was laid long before I started the business. It got a boost in late 1980, when Danielle, my wife, and I cut a deal on new career directions for me, because I was so frustrated about my work, and the lack of foresight and imagination I faced," Kevin said. "You could say I recruited her to my cause. She was my rooting section, debating opponent and partner as I shaped my business concept. It had to be something I liked doing, that would offer a decent living from meeting a developing market need, and provide real long-term value to clients. The rest was follow-through, and pushing the envelope of opportunity, until, one day, we had 45 stores."

"I read where you sold the company for more than a decent living," John Tan said, almost challenging Kevin as he said it.

"I didn't think the chain would become as big and profitable as it did, until we expanded into London with Chip Three," Kevin said. He shrugged. "Then I said, let's see how far we can push this thing, and I wrote a plan to grow to 10 stores."

"Then you were an overnight success," John said triumphantly.

"Stop this overnight success stuff," Kevin said gently. "It's somebody's fantasy, but it isn't in my experience or that of the people I know who are successes."

"Okay, but you say the first step was recruiting your wife?" Mac interjected.

"To a large degree," Kevin replied as he nodded. "All of you will have to do that, recruit your support network, starting at home. If the people you live with, who look to you for a particular type of performance, don't get it, you're sunk, because they'll make life hell for you." Kevin drummed his hands on the lectern and cocked his eyes at the ceiling, as if he were watching a movie. "The management consultant from Vancouver who helped us set up our employee training and assistance program at A Chip, when we had 10 stores, had a great way of showing how important it is to recruit your family as support network…"

He was George Macleod, with a soft Edinburgh burr to his voice, and a gentle nurturing style. He had worked as a controller for the British parent of a Canadian electronics company, and had then been sent to Canada to work at the subsidiary. The move was high stress, as most are, but George settled in quickly and went to work. The younger Macleods adjusted nicely, as children do. Mrs. Macleod took longer, but eventually adjusted too, even got herself a nice job.

After a few years, George decided he wanted to start his own business. He told his wife what he wanted to do with his life, and set up his management consultancy. To operate the company, he remortgaged their house. A year later, needing capital to expand, he announced to his wife that he needed to put a second mortgage on the house. She promptly filed for divorce, and petitioned for a court order to protect her from any liability he incurred against their house, their major joint asset. After taking time to reinvent his life, George admitted, ruefully, that not only had he not recruited his wife, he had pushed her past her comfort zone.

"His business is doing well now, by the way, and George is remarried, to someone with a higher risk tolerance level, but who requires him to continually negotiate their future with her," Kevin said. "Danielle and I operate that way. We've talked things out ever since we met at university, except for one bad patch we eventually worked through. We're also quite complementary characters. You know the story, if we were one person, we'd be a perfect person."

"I thought all successful people had no faults," John Tan called out.

Kevin stared at him, long and hard. "Do you actually believe there's something special, or different about me than you?"

John shrugged and looked uncomfortable. "A few years and a few million?" he ventured weakly.

Kevin nodded. "And that's about all. I'm just flesh and blood, like you. Anyone here made of different materials?"

The rest of the group was a little intimidated by the exchange between Kevin and John, but after some shaking of heads and soft laughter, the tension diffused.

"Back to Danielle," Kevin said. "Not only did I recruit her to my plan, but she encouraged me to leave Three C and start my own business. You see, she saw something I didn't. I was eating myself up in frustration. She proposed we use our savings and borrow the money to start A Chip Off The Old Block correctly. She was the one who suggested we reorder our household budgets to live on her teacher's salary, so, if at the end of a week there wasn't money left over after we covered all our business costs, we weren't in trouble." He stopped, and looked around the room, a mischievous twinkle in his eye. "Then we started working on my, uh, overnight success."

CHAPTER THREE

Who's in Goal?

1995, The Conference: *Morning, Day One*

The technician adjusted the microphone angle over the lectern in front of Kevin, who nodded his thanks. She threw the On switch and left the stage.

"Good morning, everyone," Kevin said to the accompaniment of a loud squeal. He waited for the sound operator's signal that the microphone volume had been adjusted. "Welcome to our first working session titled, *Defining Yourself and Your Goals*. I'm your moderator, Kevin Short. I'll keep my opening brief, then hand over to the key speaker for this session, Brenda Bashford, on my left. Next to her are Mac Sutherland, Susan Manyfingers, and John Tan—"

They nodded as their names were announced.

"—who will provide color commentary, some additional information they want to add, and participate with you in the question and answer session. Before we start, though, let's have a little fun. Please stand up and hand out, and collect, as many business cards as you can in the 30 seconds starting now."

Pandemonium ensued as people stood, and talked, and laughed as they furiously traded cards and introductions. Kevin checked off the time on his watch.

"Okay, time's up," he called. "Sit down. That was just a memory exercise, to remind you you're in business for yourself all the time, and every business card you hand out is a personalized billboard. Now, hands up if you got four cards."

Almost every hand went up.

"Seven?"

A lot fewer hands came up.

"Nine?"

Only a few hands came up.

"Twelve?"

One woman raised her hand, and Kevin looked closely at her. "Angelica Jursic. The Class of '91. Right?"

"You have a good memory, Kevin," she said in heavily accented English.

"A salesman's habit, Angelica. You win the prize, a full set of audio and video tapes of this conference. A memento, on me."

"Thank you, Kevin."

"My pleasure. Everyone, Angelica came to us to figure out how to make a business of giving English language, writing and office skills training to female immigrants from former Iron Curtain countries. How's business, Angelica?"

"In three years, I have trained 300 women, here in Toronto, but the last year of the recession, you know, made it difficult for them to get jobs quickly. However, 200 of them have found jobs here, and in Winnipeg and Vancouver, as interpreters or secretaries in businesses doing work with east European countries."

"At what, $1,000 for a 16-week course?" Kevin asked.

"$2,000," Angelica said. "And I have had full classes each time."

"Folks, Angelica is a one-person operation, does all the teaching, and contracts out the administrative work she doesn't care to handle," he said. "So how's business?"

"I am making a good living, and running a profitable business, Kevin."

Someone started applauding and the rest of the audience joined in.

"Good. Now, let's get rolling," Kevin said when the applause stopped. "Many of you who were in the program chafed when we had you go through formal career planning and counselling as part of the program. You wanted to be in business *yesterday*. Our first job was to get you to understand you needed preparation that was best done *before* you committed time and money to your venture."

There were shouts of agreement, and laughter from the audience.

"You agree with us now, but then you groaned, 'What does all this learning and planning have to do with setting up and running a business?'" Kevin's voice boomed from the PA system. "Other trainers and teachers, people in government, even people from Big Business who came to look at what we were doing, who wanted a quick, easy formula for instant success, asked the same question.

Well, Brenda Bashford, from the Class of '90, agreed to present her answer for you."

Brenda rose and walked towards the lectern.

"Brenda used the program to clarify her needs, goals, and vision and went on to create The Garden of Eatin', Vancouver's most interesting, and highly successful haute cuisine vegetarian restaurant and catering service. Folks, Brenda Bashford," Kevin said and moved aside so she could take the lectern.

Brenda shuffled her notes one more time, took a deep breath, thanked Kevin, and launched into her subject. "We're always facing new challenges in life, and the toughest challenge is taking the first step to change. Why? Because it's the biggest step, the most frightening, and the first into a new world, the unknown."

Her voice quavered at first, then settled down quickly to her warm, husky tones.

"This is true, not only in business, but in life, and particularly in life, because everything we do is a subset of life, not a substitute for it, especially the work we do, whether we do it for other people, or for our own profit. I believe this, because I have learned, if a person's life is in disarray, everything else will be in disarray. I have learned that success will always be flat, meaningless, and never enough, if we don't know, intimately, what drives our primary employees...ourselves..."

. . . .

FROM THE TRANSCRIPT OF **DEFINING YOURSELF AND YOUR GOALS**, A WORKSHOP AT THE 1995 OSWEGO COLLEGE SELF-EMPLOYMENT CONFERENCE *(Available from Allied Tape and Transcription Services Ltd., c/o Oswego College, $4.50 a copy, sales taxes included.)*

BRENDA BASHFORD: We all had to select four instructors in order of preference, and make pitches to each as to why we wanted them as our mentors. It became highly competitive, and I guess that was the point of the activity—our first lesson. Get us hungry for something important, then make us work for it. I wanted Kevin as my mentor, more than any other instructor there. I guess it was because of his simple, straight-talking, no-nonsense approach to teaching.

You have to understand that when I got into the incubator program, I was coming out of a marriage to a psychologist who had been a master at manipulation, and could make me think I was crazy, so Kevin's honest, encouraging style was quite appealing. I mean, Kevin had a simple message and stuck to it: *Business is like life, risky, but any of us can make a success out of it, if we prepare ourselves to succeed, and work for success.*

I was a new single mother, looking to design a business that would make a financially sound life for me and my son. Frankly, though, I had a problem—I didn't know who I was, and I didn't know enough to care. I had gone from my parents' home to a university residence, directly into marriage, took my CGA courses at night, had a job, full-time at first, then part-time, but I never had to be self sufficient. I guess that's why Kevin and all the other instructors in the program wanted us to look at ourselves first, to get us to understand right up front, that the only ones responsible for our successes or failures are us.

After our first mentoring sessions, we worked with the instructors who specialized in management of human resources. They guided us as we worked with formal career planning tools—workbooks, questionnaires and such—to analyze the type of people we were, how we saw the world, our definitions of success, and our skills, so we could know what we had to work on and with, how to build on our strengths, and how to overcome our weaknesses. At least they weren't those 'What are you best suited to do in life?' tests—you know, the kind that tell you you have the drive, qualifications and characteristics to be either a successful serial axe murderer or brain surgeon, or something like that.

Mind you, no one in the program ever said we didn't have what it takes to be successfully self-employed, and should or shouldn't go into business. If anything, they were like cheerleaders, always telling us we could do whatever we set out to do—anyone could—and it would be fun, *as long as we organized ourselves to do it.* Then they showed us how. Only three people dropped out in those first few weeks.

I worked part-time after Danny was born, but I wanted full-time work, and not just a job handling someone else's money, either, but something of value to me. I had a decent divorce settlement, more than I let on at that first class—and I still find it hard to believe that was only five years ago, because of all the changes I've gone through, and the way my life is going. Anyway, there was even a chance Danny's father would honor the child-support part, but I didn't want to bank on it, nor be dependent on him until Danny reaches 18. For a while, I debated whether the full-time work I could get as an accountant would provide me enough money, or the time flexibility I needed to raise Danny properly. I told myself a lot of things, but basically, I was just looking for excuses to get out of accounting. I wasn't sure what I wanted out to, but I didn't want to stay in accounting, and couldn't see it providing me the work fulfilment I needed. That's a bad place to be if you're going to be doing a job eight, 10, 12 hours a day sometimes, every day of the work week for the rest of your life.

So that first mentoring session was a form of torture. Looking at yourself in a mirror always is, especially if you're divorced, 20 pounds overweight, need to work, and desperate to get on with your life before all opportunity evaporates. Now, here I am, five years later, with something to give back...

....

1990, Fall: *A Coffee Shop At Oswego College*

"All the popular books I read, even the stuff the bank's commercial banking unit prepared for people starting up in business, say writing a plan first is the critical element for success," Mac said.

"And you believe that?" Kevin asked, putting his coffee cup down so quickly the contents sloshed over the rim.

"Well, the information is all prepared by experts," Mac said.

"And who are these experts?" Kevin wondered.

"Why, ah, lawyers, accountants, people in the commercial banking units," Mac said. "There's even stuff available from government economic development agencies in the provinces, and the federal government."

"All people who have run their own businesses, of course, who have bought and sold on their own behalf, and generated the income to pay bills, wages and such. Right?" Kevin asked, sarcasm a sour note in his voice.

"I'm not sure," Mac said, his neck reddening around his collar.

"Look, all of you," Kevin said, addressing Mac, Brenda, Susan, John, and a young woman named Anne Porter, the five people he had chosen to mentor. "I don't have all the answers. I'm learning new things every day, same as you—"

"Is that why you're always carrying that book around?" Anne asked. "You're constantly scribbling in that thing."

"The notes section of my daytimer, Anne," Kevin said.

"I'd have thought you'd carry a notebook computer," John Tan said.

Kevin smiled. "Despite my previous business, I discovered computers aren't the answer to every business need," he said as he hefted the small leather binder that bound his day book. "I do carry a sub-notebook computer, but it's time consuming to go in, find the appropriate file or routine, just to keep myself on time. This is more efficient. The computer has other applications."

"Such as...?" John prompted.

"We'll have time for that later, a whole unit on technology," Kevin said. "But this," he indicated the book again, "is a catch-all for the day's thoughts and such, until I can get to my computer, or a phone to take care of something, questions, whatever," Kevin said. "I don't trust my memory. Besides, things become more real on paper—it brings things closer to commitment, closure, reality, whatever I need."

"I don't understand," Susan said.

"Well, if you're just thinking about something, it's only happening in your head, and it's only fantasy, or a thought that can get lost," Kevin explained. "But put it on paper, and you can see it, touch it. It has substance."

Susan looked confused.

"He's talking about how things register in the subconscious," Brenda said impatiently.

"So what? You're losing me more," Susan said.

"Please, explain, Brenda," Kevin said, and sat back in his chair.

"Well, uh," Brenda shifted uncomfortably in her chair. "Oh, what the hell. I was in a weight-loss program last year, and the woman who taught it had a whole section on self-esteem issues. I learned we are the sum of our belief systems, which are the products of our personal histories and experiences, and which we hold in our subconscious minds."

"Great, so when do we light the incense, and start humming?" asked Anne irritably.

"Hang on, Anne," Mac said gently. "Let her finish before we pass judgement on the validity of what she's saying."

"I agree with Mac," Susan said. "Except I already believe it. This is the wisdom of the elders couched in modern psychobabble."

Kevin looked at Mac with deepening respect. What he had first judged to be Mac's rigidity was just quiet reserve. He might not accept new ideas easily, but he was certainly open to hearing them out. And he was glad Susan had offered her support. The key here was to be open minded.

"Thank you, both," Brenda said. "Anyway, the subconscious runs all the time, and is uncritical, so information is fed into it and isn't examined, just digested. It has no sense of time, so something programmed in there 20 years ago is just as current to the subconscious as something programmed there 20 minutes ago. The subconscious then directs our behavior accordingly."

Kevin leaned into the conversation. "The conscious mind is where we think, analyze and sort ideas, but what's there can be in conflict with the content or programming of our subconscious. Think of it this way: Your subconscious has a portrait of you shaped by your history and experience. Your conscious desire is to be a success. If your subconscious portrait doesn't portray you as successful, you will not succeed, no matter how strong your conscious desire to succeed."

"Hey! You said you don't have all the answers," John said accusingly.

"I don't," Kevin said. "But I believe this conscious-subconscious stuff. When Danielle came on board as manager of personnel and training at A Chip, we instituted a policy of continual employee training and development. I was no exception. In fact, she insisted I be a model—leadership by example. So I took a self-esteem course."

"Get out of here!" John exploded. "You? A self-esteem course?"

"Wisdom is where you find it," Kevin said. "I learn something from everybody I meet, from every course I take."

"Anyway, back to what I was saying," Brenda interrupted. "You have to see yourself as successful and enjoying success, in your subconscious and your conscious and your superconscious minds, because the subconscious is stronger than the conscious in determining how we act and perform, and the superconscious guides them both on possibilities…what we can imagine."

"Oh, I see," Anne said brightly. "You're saying writing something down makes it real to the subconscious."

"Actually, writing something down, giving it some substance as more than a thought, is a strong first step to reprogramming the subconscious," Brenda said.

"Look, this is important, but you'll be going through this with professionals in the field, and we're straying a bit from where we began, which is the question of where to start in business," Kevin interrupted. "And though I agree a business plan is critical to success, I believe in doing your personal inventory first."

"Which you, of course, as the perfect entrepreneur did. Right?" John demanded.

"No. I learned the hard way," Kevin smiled sheepishly. "Year two into the business, I was in London, Ontario, setting up our third store, so I could generate the sales volumes to get better supplier discounts, when I realized something was wrong. Store One had passed the critical hump, was surpassing second-year income projections. Store Two in downtown Toronto was a success from day one, and I was making more money than I had projected, but I felt like I was on a roller coaster, that no matter what I did, how much money came in, it wasn't enough."

"And your home life?" Mac asked.

"What home life?" Kevin said. "Danielle and I were becoming strangers. Now you can expect to work long hours in your start-up years, but I was over the top—almost obsessive about the business—and neglecting my home life, something I had never done as a salesman for Three C."

"Geez, what a shame!" Susan commented. "You were winning, but not satisfied."

"Exactly!" Kevin exclaimed. "I wasn't satisfied, because I didn't know me, what needs, what desires, what drives I was satisfying, or how they had to be satisfied. So I just worked harder and longer expecting more money would satisfy me."

"I don't get it," John said.

"Well, neither did I, until I spoke with a career counsellor, a psychologist," Kevin said. He paused a moment, and said, "You know, she helped me by showing what she had learned about herself—"

"Doctor heal thyself?" Mac asked.

"Yeah. Even psychologists have to learn to read their own life signs to understand what they're up to," Kevin nodded. "That's why I believe it's so important to understand yourself and shape your own definition of success early into the business game..."

....

Kevin had first heard Laura Gunderson on a radio talk show where she was presented as a leading expert on career planning, but Kevin was intrigued when she talked about her practice. She had associates all over North America who used, with their clients, some career-planning tools—workbooks, checklists, planners—she had developed, and he heard, behind the expert, the strong voice of a committed businessperson.

He found some articles by and about Gunderson that confirmed she was, in fact, a leader in her field. What he pieced together was a profile of a young woman who had grown up in a family of immigrant businesspeople. Her father, a sewing machine technician, had serviced and supplied businesses in Montreal's post-war textile trade; her mother had run the administrative side of the business. Laura's academic career took her from McGill University to the Sorbonne, then the University of Toronto.

The sum of her education made her all but unemployable anywhere except at a university, because corporate psychologists hadn't been invented yet. However, because of the example she absorbed from her parents, working for someone else in a job had never occurred to Laura as an option, and she wasn't interested in being an academic. When she finished her doctorate, she established herself as a general consultant in industrial psychology.

She didn't set out to create the ultimate career-planning workbook. It was just part of a professional toolbox that on its own became an important trade item. Until then, though, she was just another consulting psychologist.

"While I developed those career-planning tools, I was running a general practice in industrial psychology, and I was unhappy with most of what I did, except the career work," Laura told Kevin during their first meeting together, which he used to find out if she was the right person to help him. "But I was getting strong, positive response to the career-planning work and the materials I prepared in support of it, particularly my career-planning workbook."

As her market responded to her career-planning tools, and the associated training programs, Laura saw them as opportunities to meet her needs and goals, according to the values she held. "I never liked being second best at anything," she told Kevin. "I never want to be in a business where 20 other people could be selling what I sell." So she focused on marketing the skills and the career-planning workbook and associated materials, became better at the training and presentations, and clients responded even more positively towards her and the tools.

The next item to deal with was a matter of values. As a young married consultant, Laura had no problem about traipsing around North America doing her work. However, once she had a child, being on the road was incompatible with the values she assigned to being a good, effective parent, especially being present to raise her son, according to his needs, and not at her convenience. So she focused exclusively on further improving her career-planning training skills and materials, and developing a network of associates in North America and Great Britain who could manage, market and deliver the workbooks and training outside the geographical area in which she was prepared to travel.

Laura also came to understand herself better, and she loved developing and doing presentations. She began accepting invitations to speak at conferences and other professional development gatherings, and writing articles. "People know who I am because they've heard me speak, or they've read articles about or by me," she said to Kevin.

And, finally, she recognized she was hungry for first-rank success, and success for her was measured by a basket of yardsticks: financial rewards, respect from professional peers, and respect and admiration from her clients...

. . . .

"As her vision clarified, and her goals became clearer—and remember, this was over a few years—she redesigned her business to work to her strengths," Kevin said. "She now works from home, does her consulting in clients' offices, has her network of associates, and doesn't travel outside the Windsor-Montreal corridor if she doesn't feel like it."

"So tell us already, Kevin," John demanded. "What was your problem?"

"Oh, that," Kevin laughed. "Well, you know Central Drugs?"

"The big discount drug store chain?"

Kevin nodded. "It started in the early '50s in Toronto as a buying co-op organized by my dad. He was a pharmacist, got his education on the veteran's entitlement after the war."

"So merchandising runs in the family," Barbara said.

"Sort of," Kevin agreed. "Anyway, he had a small pharmacy on St. Clair Avenue West, which served all these immigrant communities. He saw how frugal and price conscious everyone was, and came up with the idea of discounting the sundries he carried in the store, but he could only get manufacturers' price breaks if he bought in volume. So he talked a bunch of pharmacists into buying through him, and it grew so quickly he set up a company and a big warehouse and service centre. Did well."

"He must have made a fortune when Genservco bought the chain, in '81," Mac said.

"No," Kevin said. "He sold his end of the business long before that, when he and some old war buddies got into real estate and land development deals."

"So what was your problem?" John demanded in frustration.

"Nothing spectacular," Kevin said. "I still had some growing up to do. I was measuring my success against my father's achievements, when I should have been measuring my success against my own idea of success, my own goals, which I hadn't defined for myself except as making a living with the store. So, regardless of how I was succeeding, I wasn't enjoying myself, my success, or the money, because I didn't have a true idea of what it meant to me, what it cost me, or the purpose of it all."

"That's crazy, Kevin," John said.

"I know, but we all do a lot of that, do things without knowing why," Kevin said. "Which is why, this stuff—" He pulled some papers from his briefcase and distributed three sheets to each of them. "—is so important to work out."

The top sheet read:

FIVE KEY ELEMENTS OF A PERSONAL INVENTORY

MOTIVATION

    Why are you in/going into business?

VALUES

    What is important to you in life and business?

    How do you define success?

PERSONAL ABILITIES

    What are your strengths and weaknesses?

    What do you need to change or improve?

BUSINESS ABILITIES

    What skills and experience do you have?

    What are your strengths and weaknesses?

    What do you need to change or improve?

TECHNICAL/PROFESSIONAL SKILLS

    What do you know?

    What can you do?

    What do you need to learn?

    How can you learn it?

"This is the simplified version of what I worked on with Laura. All of my potential employees answered this questionnaire as part of the employment process," Kevin said. "I wanted people on my team who were as focused as I was, and this helped us figure out if we were compatible."

"But employees come and go," Anne objected. "Isn't that an expensive way to operate?"

"No. You see, I believe that the best incentive to high performance is a vested interest in success," Kevin said. "So we set up a profit-sharing program, according to a formula based on salary, performance and the job responsibilities a person held."

"Could a high-performing, well-paid salesman make as much

as, or more than a store manager?" Susan asked.

"The responsibility, and store performance factors would always keep the manager ahead," Kevin said. "So a good part of my success with A Chip came from motivating staff with the profit sharing. Our people had a stake in the success of the business, and they acted as entrepreneurs, without having to assume business risk."

"But we're not being considered for employment by you or anyone else," Susan objected.

"Yes, you are. You're hiring yourselves," Kevin said. "You're going to be bombarded by profiling and goal setting stuff for the next two weeks, because you need to 'process yourselves'." He held up his hands to deflect complaints. "But this is the only outline you need to use, what I, and Laura, and a number of consultants who worked with A Chip Off The Old Block figured was the essential information you need to get to know yourself, and lower your risk of sabotaging your own success."

"Keep it simple, stupid. Right?" John Tan asked.

"Wrong. I hate the stupid part of the KISS model," Kevin said vehemently. "It's abusive, used by people who treat their employees like dummies. They get back splinters. I say just keep it sweet and simple. Simplicity is elegant."

"What do you want us to do with these?" Susan asked.

"Not much, except start writing answers to the questions here...to your satisfaction, and we'll just have coffee over the answers for the next few weeks, one-on-one as you need it, but also in the group," Kevin said.

"What about this?" Brenda asked, pointing to the middle page in the packet. It read:

To achieve something:
Define the goal.
Negotiate the best possible price.
Pay the price.

"There's no such thing as a free lunch," Kevin said. "This isn't to say that life is hard and then we die. Far from it. What it says, to me anyway, is that there's a price to success, and it's meaningful to us if we define what we mean by success, and decide if the price is worth the results. It's also a reminder that we are responsible for our own lives, and we can make them sweet, or we can make them sour."

"You're relentlessly positive," John said.

"It comes of following my own advice, and that of some sensible, high-priced consultants," Kevin said. "Look at the last sheet."

It read:

TO ACHIEVE GOALS

1. Define your goals.
2. Establish your focus by writing down the goals as you stated them.
3. Tighten your focus by setting dates for achieving the goals.
4. Post your goals in your high-traffic areas, and read them at least once a day, preferably three times a day—first thing in the morning, in early afternoon, and when you end the day's work.
5. Think of your goals often, and imagine yourself enjoying them.
6. Develop a plan of action.
7. Don't discuss the plan with others except your immediate family.
8. Don't follow conventional wisdom, because wisdom is rarely conventional thinking.
9. Act as though you have arrived.
10. Feel and act confident, poised and successful, and you will be.

"I put that one together over the last few years," Kevin said. "One through six came from one of those seminars Danielle sent me to. It was great. The last four I added myself."

"This is just a guide for reprogramming ourselves," Brenda said. "I saw stuff like it in my weight-loss program."

"Look, Brenda, none of this stuff, or anything you'll be going through in this program is new or groundbreaking or contains some special secret to success," Kevin said. "Every one of us has what it takes to succeed at what we do; we just haven't been trained to do it, not in school, and rarely by our families."

"Which is why there are courses and seminars on just about anything," Susan said.

"Exactly," Kevin agreed. "But what's the point of taking courses?"

"That's easy," John said. "To get you to focus on a particular task and ways to do it efficiently."

"Perfect answer," Kevin said. "Give yourself a victory lap around the college."

Everyone laughed and John shook his head.

"No, huh?" Kevin shrugged, then turned to Brenda. "This stuff will help you deal with your anxiety about getting started."

"Now you've lost me!" Brenda said.

"Look, you're in a hurry to do...what?" he asked.

"I don't know," she shrugged. "Start a restaurant. Buy a bed and breakfast place. Open a boutique."

"You've just pinpointed why you're so anxious," Kevin said. "You have no idea what you want to do, so you're eager to do *anything* just to be doing *something*. Just focus on getting your bearings, a sense of direction, purpose, goals...that's the something that needs doing now."

"If the point is to focus, why do you have number eight, the one about conventional wisdom, here?" Mac asked. "It seems out of place."

"Well, I toyed with that one for years," Kevin said. "If I had · listened to all those people at Three C who said desktop computers would never become popular, or useful in business, or displace the mainframe, I wouldn't have started A Chip Off The Old Block." Kevin paused for a long moment, and his eyes did a curious little dance, rolling up a bit, as if looking at a screen on the inside of his forehead. Then, he said, "I put it in after Black Monday, October 19, 1987."

They all looked at him blankly, then Mac said, "The stock markets..."

Susan, Brenda and John stared at Mac, then Kevin, who was grinning and nodding, then Mac again.

"The biggest single crash of stock market prices in about 60 years, since the crash that started the Great Depression," Mac said. "But I don't understand."

"Well, you see, I don't drive in downtown Toronto," Kevin said. "I usually walk or use the subway or streetcars, but..."

One day in July '87, about 12 weeks before the crash, Kevin was held up at a meeting, which made him late for another, so he hailed a cab. He settled into the seat after giving the driver the address, and was rolling some ideas over in his mind, when the cabbie's voice intruded on his consciousness.

"So, whaddaya think of the mutual funds market?" the cabbie asked.

"Excuse me?" Kevin said, mystified.

The cabbie waved a copy of the financial section of one of that day's newspapers at him. Kevin took it and saw it was folded to highlight the mutual fund price quotations.

"It's like the stock market itself, but with less risk," the cabbie said. "You can make as much money trading fund units like stocks if you buy no-load funds that are turning in high yields."

Kevin was astonished by the cabbie's remarks. "Is this a common practice these days?" he asked.

"Oh, yeah. Especially with the equity funds," the cabbie said. "The stocks are hot. The fund managers are buying and selling as fast as their computers tell them they've reached their targeted rate of return. Builds up the values of the funds quick."

"But if the fund managers are all playing the same game with computer-assisted trading, it stands to reason they'll all, at some point, reach the decision to sell at the same time, kill share values, and be left holding devalued paper."

"Naah," the cabbie insisted. "I've been following their sales meetings, you know, where they get investors in? Everybody's playing the same game. And the brokers and fund managers, they aren't stupid, they got it all under control."

In a pig's eye, Kevin thought. If everybody thinks that way, then they're all heading for the same cliff. Not only are the equity-based funds threatened, but so are the equities themselves, because they're the ones being traded according to the computer programs.

There was a public phone near the entrance of the building where Kevin was overdue for his meeting. He called upstairs and said he'd be delayed another few minutes, then he called Danielle, and quickly explained the situation. She agreed to follow his lead and inform their investment counsellors that she consented to Kevin giving them directions on her behalf. He then called the agent who handled their RRSP and mutual fund investments, and told him to put everything they held into money market funds. His next call was to their stockbroker, with instructions to roll their stock portfolios into treasury bills and other cash-based securities. Finally, he called the company's accountant and told him to liquidate the company's stock or stock-based outside investments.

In all three cases, the people he spoke with told him he should be putting more money into stock-based investments. Kevin was even more adamant about selling after hearing them out.

"And on October 19, 1987, when the Dow Jones average dropped 22.6 per cent, and the Toronto Stock Exchange's TSE 300 index dropped 11.3 per cent, billions of dollars of stock values evaporated. Everyone around me was panicking, and losing a bundle, while I went on with my business," Kevin said. "Danielle and I, and the company, didn't lose anything, not because I'm smarter than anyone else, but because I had learned not to automatically believe things because everyone else does."

....

1995, The Conference: *Brenda's Presentation*

"So working from Kevin's list, I defined my goals at that time primarily in financial terms," Brenda said. "I wanted to be running my own business, with prospects of success, within 12 months of finishing the program, with a view to achieving financial independence within five years." She turned to Kevin. "Specific enough?"

"What do you mean by financial independence?" he asked.

"The ability to save enough in tax-sheltered investments to build a retirement stake of $1,000,000," she replied.

"Specific enough," Kevin said sheepishly to everyone's laughter.

"I did select a physical goal, too," Brenda said. "To get back to my pre-pregnancy weight." She stepped from behind the lectern and turned slowly to applause from the audience. She completed the turn with a flourish, and returned to the lectern.

"It's odd, but working to achieve my physical goal was more work than achieving my business goals..."

....

BRENDA BASHFORD: I wrote those goals down, with dates and timings. Later on, when I had to work with a TV station to do ads for my restaurant, I borrowed one of their ideas, and called my goals list a script for my life. The ad people also showed me storyboards, little graphic representations of the scenes and continuity in the ads, and I borrowed from that concept and made posters using headlines and graphics I cut out from magazines to illustrate my goals, so I had pictures of them. I hung them in my bedroom and my office, and I began calling them the storyboards of my life.

Even now, if you come into my office at the restaurant, or my den at home, you'll see my goals lists prominently posted within eyesight of my desk. And I posted copies next to my bathroom mirror, on the fridge door, even on the mirror at my dressing table. I even made a small copy of the list and put it in the front of my daytimer.

I read those goals every day before I started work, at lunch, and every night before going to sleep, and I thought about them often. And I pictured myself enjoying the benefits of my work. I even went out and test drove sports cars as an incentive.

My action plan was simple. I wrote an overall business plan for my life—it was a script of what I wanted my life to be. My business plan became a part of my overall plan, as it should be. When I hit my first goal six months early, because I found an investor who seeded development funding of my concept of a gourmet vegetarian restaurant, I learned that good plans have to be flexible and revisable. So, when a projected timeline ran longer than I expected, I didn't feel like a failure. Rather, I just accepted that sometimes things take longer to achieve. It also gave me room to accept that some goals might appear attractive, but aren't necessarily so when examined closely. Sometimes, it makes sense to bail out of a course of action to save wasted effort, and doing so doesn't make a person a failure.

I talked the plans over with my Aunt Jane, the one everyone says is eccentric, but who is actually just interesting, and has a good analytical head. She never tells me what I should do, but rather asks me questions about my needs, wants, and options. And I followed my instincts on decisions, rather than doing what other people told me I should do. Mind you, I did my homework, and researched any issues that affected me but that I didn't understand.

All of you who have started businesses will probably have lists of people who said you couldn't or shouldn't do what you're doing. If we had listened, where would we be? In my case, doing nothing. Everyone told me I was crazy to open a *haute cuisine* vegetarian restaurant.

My research told me Montreal, Toronto, and Vancouver had sufficient populations with the attitudes that would support my plan. I opted for Vancouver, because of the weather. Now, people from Montreal, Toronto, and Calgary want to buy franchise rights to The Garden of Eatin'.

Finally, thanks to this program, I was able to go out and face my fears about success and failure. All the time, I believed I was succeeding. I was prepared, and became stronger for it. I had faith in myself, and I knew no matter who bought into my ideas, or didn't buy in, I had to believe with all my heart, soul and being that I was getting what I wanted and needed out of life, and that it was all of value.

Today, I have my restaurant, and a good foundation for the security I was looking for. My son is happy, healthy and getting a good education, and has a happy mother who contributes positively to his life. Not only that, but at nine, he's being taught to cook by the best vegetarian chef in the country. And why is that important? Well, cooking is a good skill for anyone to have, but in Danny's case, it's an important survival skill.

You see, my decision to start a vegetarian restaurant was based on many considerations—financial, personal, and health. Danny has all these food allergies, and the best way to deal with them was for both of us to adopt a vegetarian lifestyle. The progression seemed natural. Now, here's a bonus to the story. We have a strong vegetarian clientele, but another, unexpected market segment that developed quickly and strongly for us is people with food allergies, simply because we created menus sensitive to those people, and we ran a small two-line disclaimer about allergies on our menus and in all of our advertising, promotional and public relations materials. That's why a group of investors thinks it can sell the concept of an upscale vegetarian restaurant in Calgary, the beef capital of Canada.

CHAPTER FOUR

Find Your Own Business

1995, The Conference: *Morning, Day One, Coffee Break*

Kevin ended his call and slipped the phone into his pocket as he returned to the conference hall. Danielle had everything under control, though she had to chase down their lawyer at his retreat somewhere in cottage country, but the plan was in place and Kieron's Sunday Surprise, as they had dubbed their little conspiracy, was ready. He was so looking forward to his brother's expression when it was unveiled, and had even booked a video cameraman for the event.

The vision was so amusing and engrossing that Kevin almost ran right over the slight, dark-haired woman who moved into his path.

"Mr. Short, I am Monique Pelletier," she said with just a hint of a French accent as she handed him her card.

Kevin quickly read it. Ms. Pelletier was with the Secretary of State, one of the conference's sponsors. At last count, there were four federal ministries, and at least two from each province and territory represented at the conference.

"Please, call me Kevin," he said and handed her his card.

"Yes, Kevin, and call me Monique," she said, pocketing the card. "I am with the steering committee on small business development and I wanted to know what you think we could do better to help develop small business in Canada."

Kevin laughed. "Monique, do you have a week...maybe the time to wait while I write a book...?" he asked.

"Surely you could tell me briefly..."

"Monique, I could give it to you in a few wholly inadequate sentences, or I could document situation after situation, which would bore you to tears."

"Please, the few wholly inadequate sentences, to start," she said. "Then, perhaps you could come to Ottawa to speak with me."

"Okay, Monique, it's like this. We have many people in this country with the guts, determination, vision, desire, and drive to start and build businesses. We have the educational, services, and technological infrastructures necessary to make any business fly."

"Then why do we have trouble developing businesspeople?" Monique demanded.

"Because most of our people are not disposed to go into business, because they were neither raised, nor educated, to see being in business is a reasonable, decent, honorable and effective way to make a living. Nor are they prepared by our educational, cultural and social institutions to be in business," Kevin said with exasperation. "To help small business develop, we must present business skills and business perspectives to people as life skills, and nurture those skills…and the right attitude—an attitude of independence and social responsibility. We also have to show them businesspeople aren't all necessarily just some corporate nobility exploiting workers or consumers. We must help them learn, and achieve, their potential for being in business."

"Breathtakingly simple," Monique said. "Change our entire society and culture."

"If that's what it takes, fine," Kevin said. "A lot of traditional power brokers will have to give up a bit of control. Most importantly, we all have to acknowledge the world is changing, and at least half the businesses and jobs available 20 years from now will be things we never imagined."

"But to finance this revolution…" Monique pursed her lips and shrugged. "What about money?"

Kevin thought a moment, and said, "For business needs, it's hard to get money from our conservative investment community, but not impossible. Though you could prod the banking community to put more of its profits back into Canadian businesses on an investment basis. Better still, get governments out of the business of financing business, and trying to pick winners. Redirect your efforts into developing efficient ways for business and small investors to finance business development."

"The American model," she said with obvious distaste.

"No, not the American model," Kevin shook his head. "An entrepreneurial model, which encourages people to risk capital in ventures which offer returns that will compensate for the risks, and reward their patience."

"That would never work here," she countered.

"As long as people think that's the case, it won't work here, because no one will take the necessary risks."

"And you? Have you acted on this theory of yours?" she asked slyly.

He looked at her for a moment, then shook his head. "No theory, Monique. The reality of business is nothing like you think it is," he said.

"So, you have not acted on this theory," she said triumphantly.

"On the contrary," Kevin said. "There are seven people in that conference hall today—and I won't tell you who, because it's no one's business but ours and theirs—in whom my wife and I have invested a little more than two million dollars of our own money."

She almost looked disappointed.

"The key, Monique, is to break with convention," Kevin said. "The conventional ways of doing business don't work any more. They're destroying this country."

. . . .

FROM THE TRANSCRIPT OF **THE BUSINESS OF CHOICE**, A PANEL DISCUSSION AND WORKSHOP AT THE 1995 OSWEGO COLLEGE SELF-EMPLOYMENT CONFERENCE *(Available from Allied Tape and Transcription Services Ltd., c/o Oswego College, $15 a copy, sales taxes included)*

MAC SUTHERLAND: There were times in the incubator environment when I found Kevin a little hard to take. I thought at first it was his informality. I guess I was expecting some guy in a three-piece suit who would speak in slow, measured tones about everything, and sound like the foundation, if not the pillar, of society. Instead, we got this high-energy, animated guy who fenced with us all the time. He was quick on his feet, had a sharp mind honed by experience, and had nothing to prove to anyone.

Maybe he was too, well, dismissive of authority to please me, but I've spent most of my life in tightly organized authority systems— the military, law enforcement, and the banking world—so, I look back now and understand my initial resistance to him. Now that I've been on my own, though, running my own show, well, Kevin doesn't seem irreverent so much as realistic. I've discovered that a lot of people who were supposed to be great businesspeople really aren't.

How do I know? The security business is booming these days. What with budget cuts all over the country, shrinking police forces, and the like, the services my company provides are in great demand. Given the cuts in police and military budgets, I also have a large pool of trained talent to dip into for my operatives. We've doubled in size twice since 1990, and we're due for expansion again. All of this growth has been fuelled primarily from cash flow. I was concerned that as soon as I was a private operator, my old contacts would shut me out. Nothing could have been further from reality. Thanks to word-of-mouth, I had two major corporate clients, and one of the credit card service bureaus as clients before I had even rented an office.

My business has two components, protection and investigation. We gather information in the course of our business, and you wouldn't believe what we learn about our clients. Client confidentiality prevents me from saying anything specific, except you'd be surprised how many corporate emperors are wearing no clothes. Now there's the difference between Kevin and me. He'd have choice, colorful things to say about them; I've heard a few of them over the past five years. I still hold some respect, however shredded, for the office, if not the office holder.

Anyway, I wasn't in as much of a hurry as Brenda to get going in business, because I had a time and money buffer. Actually, given what I learned in the banking world, in the incubator, and since, I figure anyone desperate to get into a business yesterday has bigger problems than unemployment. Which isn't to say there aren't other ways of getting into business than the way we did it, as we found out when we did some team analysis of the different methods of doing business.

The instructors had all, in a moment of rare agreement, broken down the range of business operations for the delivery of goods or services to: FRANCHISES; MULTI-LEVEL MARKETING; MANUFACTURING; RETAILING; SERVICE PROVIDING AND PROFESSIONAL SERVICES. We then had to team-research these operations, and examine their pros and cons, and present a report on each to the group.

Kevin was concerned that we not lose sight of the important issue for people going into business, which is that we must have a product or a service to commercialize, and our primary task is to sell, and that business operations are just delivery mechanisms. He trotted out one of his stories to illustrate.

When he had the computer chain, he was on one of his cross-country, 'visit the stores, meet and greet' trips. On these trips he would work the floor, just fitting in, and studying the dynamics of each store. A fellow in Kitchener wanted a laptop computer, and as was (and still is) his habit, Kevin got into a conversation with the client, asked about his family, business...the way you would speak with a friend over coffee. I think that's why Kevin is so good at selling. He's curious about everything, and is really easy with people. When he asks you about yourself, you just know he's giving you his undivided attention out of a genuine interest in you and what you're up to. He makes you want to give him your business because you feel good about doing it, and you know you will get value in many different ways. I can't do that. I like to reassure people that I'm the best person for the job, and their problems will now be under control.

Anyway, this fellow worked as an aromatherapist, which, the best I understand it, means he treats people for physical and emotional ailments with scents rendered from plants, herbs and other natural sources. I don't question this stuff any more. Heck, I even bought into the subconscious stuff and took a meditation course at the Yoga Institute in Toronto. I don't understand it all, but it's as focused and disciplined an approach to life as anything I learned bashing around a parade square in the army.

This aromatherapist sold his essences by mail, supplied some to a perfumer in New York, and even consulted to and supplied businesses by providing them with scents that made work and business places more attractive environments. He had, however, originally identified and targeted a 'New Age' market large enough to support a profitable business, and overall, from all of his markets, he was really making big dollars from his scents. (John Tan came up with that one.) Kevin found out the aromatherapist was making a decent living when they worked through different scenarios for financing a computer purchase, including leasing. Then his customer decided to pay in cash.

Anyway, about that research project, and you have the results in the information packages you were given at the door: I think each group did a good job on its topic. The reports were like small books, full of research data, charts, graphs and other information. The executive summary of each report focused on eight points the group leaders agreed were important for consistent judging of the business operations, and the reports. The points we considered were: Start-up/Capital Investment; Competitive Advantage; Autonomy of Operations; Paperwork Burden; Contact With Public; Inventory Requirements; Risk Level; Freedom of Movement of Individual. Together they created a portrait of each of the businesses analyzed that showed what it cost to get in, operate and stay in business.

Kevin said the time to examine the types of businesses available was after we had done our personal inventories and goal setting, but before we prepared our business plans. This way, given that we had analyzed what we were prepared to put into a business, and what we needed out of it, we could make better decisions about what type of business to get into. Another way he had of explaining it was: "If all your experience is as a retailer, you just might go into retailing as a matter of habit, not because it serves your needs and purposes. Yet, it might turn out that you're more suited to running a manufacturing operation that serves the retail sector you've worked in before." In the case of at least one person from the Class of '90, he was bang on target.

. . . .

TEAM ONE, FRANCHISE REPORT, OCTOBER 1990
EXECUTIVE SUMMARY

INTRODUCTION
Franchises represent the simplest entry opportunity to business for those who have never been in business for themselves. They also offer potentially lower-risk opportunities for those who feel the need to get into business quickly, but feel intimidated, or overwhelmed, by the prospect of learning how to establish a business from scratch.

Franchises can be bought as start-ups, or established (turnkey) franchises being resold. Franchisees are generally buying business, product, presence, and market knowledge and experience accumulated by the franchiser in setting up the original business.

This is the most important benefit of buying a franchise: a newcomer to business can reduce the risk he or she faces in business, and avoid costly mistakes, if the franchisee follows a proven franchiser's plan.

Information about franchising is available through franchise directories available from bookstores and at libraries, and franchise trade shows held across the country. Franchise regulation varies dramatically from province to province, so potential franchisees should research any claims made by franchisers based in other provinces.

START-UP/CAPITAL INVESTMENT

Franchise fees and licences start as low as a few thousand dollars, and go up from there depending on the franchise track record and product line or service. Costs of franchiser-supplied equipment, signage, and advertising can be substantial. If a franchise is in a retail location, the franchiser usually either owns the property, or holds the property lease, so the franchisee only pays rent. This is often another profit point for the franchiser.

The key issue to watch for is whether royalties and other fees paid to the franchiser on an ongoing basis are compensated for, and exceeded, by the savings that come from central or group buying price breaks.

COMPETITIVE ADVANTAGE

Franchises offer product and name recognition and visibility, familiarity on the part of consumers with the product and product line, and the expectation of consistency and predictability in product, quality, price and service. The client's comfort zone is potentially high due to familiarity with the name and product.

AUTONOMY OF OPERATIONS

The franchisee is buying experience and centralized development of product lines. Because a key competitive advantage to franchises is consistency and predictability in product, quality, price and service, little or no deviation from standard product lines and operating procedures is allowed.

PAPERWORK BURDEN

Franchisees are responsible for administering: all wages and salaries;

all sales taxes, where applicable; unemployment insurance; Workers' Compensation contributions; government pension plan deductions, where applicable; employee health plans; other private insurance plans (if any); federal and provincial income taxes (paid quarterly); annual returns.

Franchisees must ensure municipal business licences are current, and pay municipal business taxes and/or other fees.

Franchisees must regularly fill out reports, requisitions, and remittances to the franchiser. If a franchise is in a mall, reports might also be required by mall management, which often gets a percentage of a franchise's income, through the leaseholder, who is usually the franchiser.

CONTACT WITH PUBLIC
Franchises deal in highly visible products or services acquired directly by consumers, so contact with the public is direct and high.

INVENTORY REQUIREMENTS
Inventory requirements vary according to the type of franchise.

RISK LEVEL
The 'turnkey' nature of franchises, the low learning curve, franchiser-provided operations and policy manuals, group-buying power, and competitive advantages offer generally lower business risk.

FREEDOM OF MOVEMENT OF INDIVIDUAL
Franchises are most profitable when there is a high degree of participation and direct management by the franchisee. Franchise agreements usually spell out the franchisee's responsibilities.

. . . .

FROM THE TRANSCRIPT OF **THE BUSINESS OF CHOICE**, A PANEL DISCUSSION AND WORKSHOP AT THE 1995 OSWEGO COLLEGE SELF-EMPLOYMENT CONFERENCE

PAUL BURNHAM: I wasn't part of the franchise research group, but I could see the moment I read the report they loved the concept.

So did I. No-pain, no-risk business is what it seemed like, but, like the saying goes, if it sounds too good to be true, it probably is. This doesn't mean that there's high risk to franchises. Kevin just wanted us to take a realistic look at them, because franchises are generally low-risk, but not no-risk ventures.

He had told us about a guy in Calgary named Mike Tesch, an engineer who had bought a donut franchise, and I spent a fair amount of time on the phone with him, asking about his experience of franchising. Tesch was satisfied. The franchise business had met his need to make a living and achieve financial security, and had given him a chance to learn about running a business while doing it, and being able to call on the expertise of the franchiser when necessary.

Actually, I spoke with a lot of people who had different food, and other goods and service franchises. They all loved the franchise system. I also noticed that a lot of new franchise owners were people who had lost their jobs in big businesses. Their only common concern was the degree to which the franchisers controlled the product and pricing. While franchisers do this to ensure consistency in quality, service and identity across the country, it doesn't allow the franchisee much latitude for independent action, such as introducing additional products or services that might meet a local demand.

I didn't think that would be a problem when I decided I wanted to buy a music store franchise. I had worked since my teens in record stores and the tape and record, then tape, CD, and video departments of discount and department stores. I got my first department manager's job in 1982, but from 1984 to 1989, I lost two jobs as manager in different department stores because they were reducing staff. I was ready to fit into a business that offered a stable, quiet, low-risk comfort zone, and, well, if you own the franchise, who's going to lay you off? So, in '91, after the Oswego program, I borrowed enough money from my family and got two friends to back me in buying an established Sounds Good franchise in Winnipeg.

The franchise had long dominated the retail trade for music products in a downtown location. At first, we made good money there. I only had one competitor in the area, also a chain store, but this one was owned and operated by its parent. We engaged in a genteel competition, ran specials, and other promotions as allowed by our parent companies, but, basically, we shared a market large enough to support the two of us, and revenues from the franchise remained high. Through careful management on my part, everyone was paid out within 18 months, and you can be assured I made a comfortable living. By the middle of 1994, our third year, what with bonuses and the like, I also was building some respectable RRSP and other savings. Then an aggressive, growing discount chain stormed into town and set up a company-owned store down the street, and declared war, fighting with low profit margins and chopped prices.

I was unable to compete on price and lost 50 per cent of my business in two weeks. You can't imagine what it's like to see your numbers shrink that much that quickly, and I don't suggest it's something you wish to experience.

My franchiser wouldn't give me any support in the battle by letting me move outside the rigid pricing program stage-managed from Toronto for the entire chain. Worse still, imagine this: When I told the president of the franchising company this was the start and we were in for some real combat, and asked what he was going to do to help me stay competitive, he shrugged, and said he had some advice. "Duck!" he said. Duck! He dismissed the problem as temporary, while suggesting buyers were just responding to the novelty of the new seller's deep-discount ploys to capture market share. He reassured me the discounter would eventually have to raise his prices, and we could all share the market.

I wanted to know what planet he and his head-office people were on. The new kid on the block, Tunesmiths, was killing my business, and wasn't going to give up until I shut down. I held on for two more months, each week sending Toronto sales reports that backed up my written pleas to the franchiser for help, which were ignored, or resulted in the most ridiculous memos I've ever read to justify leaving me dangling in the wind, while still paying 6.5 per cent of my gross income to the franchiser.

So I went and rented a store in a shopping mall, and set it up with racks and other fixtures. Concurrently, I had my employees pack up the inventory I had paid for, and move it in stages to the mall store.

One Sunday, we papered over the windows of the franchise store and put up a notice that it was closed for renovations. That was on the advice of my lawyer, so no one could say I had abandoned the franchise or location. Then we moved the rest of the inventory and equipment, and reopened the next day, at 10 a.m., 15 minutes after a statement of claim was delivered to the franchiser in Toronto, claiming damages because the franchiser had violated the letter and spirit of the franchise agreement by not providing appropriate corporate support to my franchise to ensure its competitiveness, and had, in fact, by its actions limited my ability to compete. It was a calculated risk. They could have bound me up in expensive legal wrangling for years, except, as I had hoped, and my lawyer concurred, the franchiser figured if the issue of corporate support for local or regional conditions had gone to court, legions of their franchisees would have revolted for the same reason I had. Better to cut me a quiet deal than fight all of the franchisees.

The franchiser bought back the franchise, and I was released from my franchise obligations, and they didn't require a non-disclosure agreement from me, which shows you how sloppy their management is. The franchiser turned the store into an owned and operated unit it will keep going until the lease is up. They're still losing money. Me, I'm a happy camper. I just opened my second independent Sonic Tonic store, and I have moments of an entertaining fantasy in which I grow my company big enough to buy the franchiser, and fire the president.

. . . .

TEAM TWO, MULTI-LEVEL MARKETING REPORT, OCTOBER 1990
EXECUTIVE SUMMARY

INTRODUCTION
Multi-Level Marketing (MLM) has been a business method employed in commerce for more than 40 years. It is sometimes confused with pyramid selling, an illegal business practice. MLM is, however, legal, because its purpose is to sell products to the public. An MLM operating structure is, however, pyramidic, and each person in the structure is, essentially, self employed.

People are recruited to sell some sort of product, and generally have to buy a package of goods up front as samples or goods for sale. It's a cash business, generally operated from the home, with further goods ordered as sales are made with rebates, discounts and bonuses computed on volume of sales. In rare situations, an MLM might require hefty inventory investments at the front end.

Besides selling, each person in an MLM network is usually encouraged to recruit other people to sell more of the product. The incentive is that a portion of the sales made by new recruits in these networks moves upward to the people who recruited them. In MLM operations, some people make more money from their cut than from their own sales. These people, however, work with their recruits, motivating and often teaching them how to sell the product.

The continual recruiting for MLM networks is the cause of its major criticisms. Hundreds must be recruited for the strong performing self starters to emerge, and many who don't make large amounts of money from their work, or actually make very little, often feel cheated and claim the MLM made fraudulent promises. The MLM industry, however, is predicted to become a major method for selling and delivering quality goods to consumers at significant savings over the next decade, because it cuts out the warehousing and transportation overheads that are included in the prices of goods sold through conventional retail outlets.

It must be noted that opportunities to enter and do well in MLM are greater the newer, or 'younger', the MLM network and product. The older, or more mature, the network, the more the market for its product has been penetrated, and the more 'territories' have been carved up among sellers. These mature MLM networks tend to be crowded with sellers who have their regular and loyal clients.

A variation on the MLM is the home-party selling system, in which 'salespeople' buy presentation inventories which they display at sales parties. The party attendees can buy the samples, or order more for later delivery. Recruiting of others in a multi-level system isn't necessarily a characteristic of home-party selling, but does happen if the home-party system is a characteristic of the MLM.

START-UP/CAPITAL INVESTMENT
The buy-in cost is usually low, in the few hundred dollar range, rarely more than $1,500. MLM is generally a cash business, with customers buying, paying up front and the seller sending in prepaid orders to efficient distribution systems that ensure delivery in short

order. Aggressive sellers often buy inventory when they've established a territory and clientele, so they can supply clients on demand.

COMPETITIVE ADVANTAGE

The people who benefit the most in the MLM system are those who have recruited large numbers of people into the network who buy from them the goods they then sell to their clientele. A highly motivated person can likely earn any targeted income, by working aggressively to achieve the target.

There are few middlemen and high-cost overheads such as transportation and warehousing between the manufacturer and sellers in an MLM, so prices to the consumer of high-quality goods can be lower than they would be for comparable items in department stores. Direct service in client homes makes this the most personal of businesses.

AUTONOMY OF OPERATIONS

Essentially, MLM operators at the regional level and below are on their own, which is why they build networks amongst themselves, and have regular promotional and motivational meetings, often with the participation of other high performers in the network brought in to speak.

Despite the built-in support system, many people try to go it on their own as MLM operators. There does not appear to be statistical evidence to support one side or another in the argument that there is only one effective MLM model. Playing within the network system isn't as critical to doing business in this environment as is the determination to make money at selling something. This means the operator—player or not—must be a strong self starter with deep motivation to tackle this type of selling.

PAPERWORK BURDEN

Paperwork includes: general administrative work with suppliers in the network; managing income and expense records for federal and provincial income and sales taxes. These operations fall into many grey areas because of the diversity of municipal and provincial licensing. Potential operators should check with local authorities about regulations.

CONTACT WITH PUBLIC

MLM is direct sales—going after clients to ask for their business—so contact with the public is intense and constant. Because of the bad name MLM networks have, there is some consumer resistance to doing business with MLM operators. Once sold, though, buyers tend to be loyal and regular. This makes MLM networks that provide quality consumable goods at better than competitive prices, delivered directly to the consumer, attractive to some people.

INVENTORY REQUIREMENTS

Generally low, unless the operator is serving a large network, then, however, product turns over rapidly.

RISK LEVEL

MLM operations generally require low up-front cash and inventory requirements. The risk remains low if the operator develops a client and income base while living on another income. The risk can be high if an operator turns to MLM as a main income source before building a client base, or makes large inventory purchases before clients buy.

FREEDOM OF MOVEMENT OF INDIVIDUAL

MLM operators rarely operate from offices, stores, or warehouses, but use their homes and cars for their business.

....

FROM THE TRANSCRIPT OF **THE BUSINESS OF CHOICE**, A PANEL DISCUSSION AND WORKSHOP AT THE 1995 OSWEGO COLLEGE SELF-EMPLOYMENT CONFERENCE

ANNA-MARIA GIZMONDI: I love working with people. I love talking with them, motivating them, hearing what they have to say. You need that kind of attitude if you want to make it in multi-level marketing, because, if you want to make big money, you need to have a small army of people, in a sense, working for you. Now that might sound strange, because we all know people in MLM networks aren't employees or anything like that. I'll explain, but I want to backtrack a bit, first.

Before I got into MLM, I worked in retail clothing after I left high school. Over 10 years, I had four jobs. Doesn't sound like I had much career continuity, or success, does it? Well, you're right, but here's the odd part: I kept getting let go because I was good at my job, which was selling clothes. I worked for Patches, the jeans people, The Co-ed Shop, Lady Lively, and Blue Eyes. The first two times I was let go, I was devastated. I mean I had the highest sales of any person in my stores. I even won chain-wide competitions for monthly sales performance a number of times. I even got along with my co-workers. So why was I being fired?

One of my friends from Patches told me. I was too successful, which threatened the store manager. She thought head office might decide to offer me her job, so I was turfed. I found out from a friend at The Co-ed Shop that I had been fired for the same reason. It didn't make the sting of the job loss any better, let me tell you. Nor did it make it any easier when the same thing happened at Lady Lively.

While I was working at Blue Eyes, the lingerie chain store, I went to a house party a friend hosted for a lingerie MLM called For Your Eyes Only, and I was impressed by the product. It was high quality, beautifully designed, and priced about 20 per cent lower than anything of comparable quality being offered at Blue Eyes. I didn't think much about the MLM thing, though, except that I had heard it was bad business, and a rip-off. But then, as year-end '89 approached, and the third quarter sales results were posted, I was the chain's top-selling employee for three consecutive quarters. One more quarter, and I stood to get a big bonus, and my own store to manage.

Then the pattern started to repeat itself. My manager began picking at me for little things, blaming me for things that were going wrong in the store, and putting it all in memos to me with copies to head office. I didn't wait for her game to play out. I quit.

Instead of looking for a job, I called the friend who had hosted the For Your Eyes Only party, and asked for the name and number of the woman from the MLM. She had been recruiting that night, but back then I hadn't been interested. Now, though, I figured from the way she had talked, maybe in the MLM I could make for myself the kind of work environment and income that recognized and rewarded success, that I couldn't get in the conventional workplace. So I called that woman from For Your Eyes Only, bought a sample case, and went to work, ready to conquer the world. I worked hard...and barely made my expenses.

I was devastated, but I had no idea what I had done wrong. I decided to give it up, and open my own store, but though I could sell, I didn't know about store and business management. I had heard about the Oswego program, and talked my way into the first class of 20.

Like I say, I had been thinking of opening a women's clothing store, but that was the height of the recession in Toronto, where I live. The city needed another women's clothing store like I needed a pet shark. Then we did the business opportunities reports and I worked on the MLM report.

That's when I figured out what I had done wrong in the For Your Eyes Only MLM. If I wanted to make a decent living, I had to reach a large number of prospective customers. The secret was in being a distributor supplying a network of sellers I recruited and motivated. Life is good; I had my answer. I wasn't selling lingerie, I was selling people on the idea of selling lingerie I sold them. I went back to work with my For Your Eyes Only sample case, even as I continued in the program here.

I started by getting my friends to host parties and invite their friends, and I was aggressive about recruiting new people, because, as their 'distributor', I got a percentage of the total sales they generated, including the sales of people they recruited into their networks, and it moves that way down through the levels of marketing. The lingerie MLM network system works on groups of 10 as distribution systems. I run five of them.

I then began looking around for a costume jewellery MLM, as a complement to the lingerie lines, and found one. I drew the people from my lingerie MLM into the jewellery line.

Now, I'm successful at this, because I've looked for people who want to make some money, but can't or won't commit to a full-time business, who like to interact with other people, and are open, outgoing people themselves. I spend a lot of time with them over coffee, and we have little network parties. I like the people I work with, and nurture them, praise them, share their victories with them, cry with them about their losses, and sympathize with them about their boyfriends or husbands, or whatever, and celebrate their ability to sell. They give me back, personally, what I give them. They've made me financially secure, and I never hold it against any of them that they can sell more than me. Why should I? I make money from their sales. Of course I'm glad they can sell more than me!

How glad? In 1993, I made $60,000 and didn't sell anything to an end user. This year, I've added a line of all cotton casual clothing and beach wear. If I keep on at the pace I'm going now, I should gross about $95,000 this year. And no one is going to fire me for succeeding. If anything, they give me awards and rewards. I like MLM.

. . . .

TEAM THREE, MANUFACTURING REPORT, OCTOBER 1990
EXECUTIVE SUMMARY

INTRODUCTION
Manufacturing is the most expensive, labor-intensive business opportunity. This business requires sizeable capital outlays, a reliable production and sales force, land, buildings, equipment, access to price-competitive raw materials and transportation to markets. The administrative burden is high and includes permits, easements, worker health and industrial safety, Workers' Compensation guidelines and documentation, environmental safety approval, unemployment insurance, federal and any private or provincial pension plans.

A manufacturing operation also requires expertise in the particular production processes for which a plant is designed.

If the reason for considering building a plant is to make a particular product, the businessperson could avoid heavy capital investments, and other up-front and operating costs by contracting out all or part of the manufacturing, packaging, sales and distribution.

START-UP/CAPITAL INVESTMENT
Capital outlays to construct and operate a plant—for land, buildings, equipment, raw materials, production staff, sales staff—can run into millions of dollars. Buying an existing plant and converting it would still be an expensive proposition.

65

COMPETITIVE ADVANTAGE

Competitive advantage is hard to establish for manufacturers in North America. The major competitive issues facing North American industry are high labor costs and operating in an environment with an expensive cost of living.

The manufacturer does, however, control the means of production, research and development. If the manufacturer is running a contract plant, producing goods to client specifications, the advantage is the manufacturer's ability to produce a high-quality, competitively priced product.

AUTONOMY OF OPERATIONS

An independent manufacturing facility is the owner's biggest asset, but can also be the biggest liability. Management must be organized and disciplined to manage the operation and staff. Leadership, management and cost controls must be balanced to motivate staff to generate high levels of low-cost productivity.

PAPERWORK BURDEN

The administrative burden is high. Besides operational details covered in this summary, a manufacturer is responsible for administration of: unemployment insurance, Workers' Compensation premiums; federal pension plan participation; employee health plans, and other private insurance plans (if any); federal and provincial income, sales, or other value-added taxes (paid quarterly); annual returns; municipal business licences and business taxes.

A manufacturer must also be concerned with long-term product liability. Overall, the administrative burden and North American labor costs make manufacturing prohibitively expensive here, unless an operation depends heavily on computerization and robotics. This increased-efficiency productivity model, however, severely limits the purchasing power of populations in former processing-based economies. The more people get laid off, the fewer there are to buy the products.

The trend to knowledge businesses means North Americans will have to change their vision of manufacturing from turning rock into cars, to turning environmentally friendly ideas into money. This means learning to conceive of a recording studio, an artist's work loft, a businesswoman's office-in-a-computer, the one-person design shop, the consultant's office, a millwright's machine shop, as a manufacturing plant—a place where products are made, or services shaped for sale to consumers.

CONTACT WITH PUBLIC
A manufacturer's contacts with the public are generally low intensity. A manufacturer might have to deal with distributors, or buyers for stores or chains, but, typically, there are many people between the manufacturer and the buying public.

INVENTORY REQUIREMENTS
Manufacturers can organize for 'just in time' delivery programs to cut the investment of time, money and space to acquire, hold and store goods for processing, but, generally, inventory requirements can be high. Successful manufacturers learn to pace production, so they aren't holding large amounts of unsold inventory.

RISK LEVEL
A manufacturer's risk level is high in terms of front-end cash outlays for land, plant, equipment, supervisory and operating staff development, market development, and sales staff.

FREEDOM OF MOVEMENT OF INDIVIDUAL
A large part of a manufacturer's life and fortune is tied in to a physical plant in a particular location. This requires the operator's presence on a regular and consistent basis to protect the interests of any and all investors.

. . . .

FROM THE TRANSCRIPT OF THE **BUSINESS OF CHOICE**, A PANEL DISCUSSION AND WORKSHOP AT THE 1995 OSWEGO COLLEGE SELF-EMPLOYMENT CONFERENCE

STAN EVERETT: I went to work at The Grange as a management trainee when I left university with my Bachelor of Commerce degree. I worked in sporting goods, small housewares, men's shoes, then men's clothing, and I enjoyed the clothing department the most. I became department head, then a junior buyer for men's casuals, and was senior chain buyer for men's casuals, in line to be head buyer for all men's clothing and accessories, when I was laid off.

I had liked my job. I have a good feel for men's clothing, and I liked the travel and variety of experiences that come with being a buyer. I wanted to stay in the buying business, but after a year of going after jobs with clothing chains, and not being able to get more than a salesman's job, I was dispirited. I came here because I figured if I was going to sell men's clothing, it would be from my own store, but I needed to learn about setting up and running a business.

I was in the group that did the retailing report, but when I read the manufacturing report I remembered Joe Spiegel, a Montreal hatmaker I had met at a clothing trade show. In the mid-'80s, when he was looking to broaden his product lines, he set up a joint venture with Astral Shirt Co. of New York to make budget-priced work shirts, the 'wear, wear out, and rip to rags' kind that could retail between US$8 and US$10 in the U.S., and between Cdn$9 and Cdn$11 in Canada.

Spiegel ran the Canadian market, and Astral took care of the U.S. market. The material and findings were American made, and the textiles were bulk cut to patterns in a range of sizes in a contract shop in the southwestern U.S., then shipped to Panama where they were assembled and shipped according to invoices and shipping slips provided by Joe and Astral. Because the materials content was 100 per cent American, and Panama had Most Favored Nation (MFN) trading status, there were no duties or taxes charged on the finished products coming into the United States or Canada.

Now here's where the major risk of contracting out—not having direct control of the process, including quality control—came into play. Joe and his partner worked with the Panamanian contractors until internal political strife over the Noriega regime made the Panamanian operation unviable. The contract work was moved to Haiti, which also had MFN status, but the quality of the finishing work, and the general reliability of shipping and handling of the finished products, deteriorated drastically. Though the partnership had made substantial profits over the years it operated, Joe lost patience after a few months of working with the Haitian contractor, the mounting time demands that diverted him from his core business, and general frustration that resulted from quality and delivery problems. He decided to leave the partnership, and look for other, less complicated, ways of diversifying his product lines.

I called Joe, as a courtesy, to ask whether he minded if I contacted Astral about becoming its Canadian partner. Joe not only said he didn't mind, but if I was serious about the idea, he would bankroll me, as long as he didn't have to have any hands-on participation. We cut a deal over the phone, and I faxed him a draft copy of the formal letter of agreement. Soon, we were sending documents back and forth while I dealt with Astral, first by phone, then directly, when I went to New York.

I knew the Astral boss, Benny Twigg, from trade shows and other sales meetings, and he remembered me, and he was eager to have a new partner. He had moved the manufacturing back to Panama after the U.S. invaded to arrest Noriega and it became relatively safe to do business there again. I suggested we also look to China for production, and asked John Tan and his cousin to act as our intermediaries in preparing a list of people we needed to get to know in China, and setting up meetings and such with them.

Astral and I now own a company called Pique A-Boo Shirts, a manufacturer without physical-plant overheads. We manufacture high-quality, low-cost shirts for our own Peak (up to Cdn$15), Too Right (up to Cdn$25) and Topper (up to Cdn$45) labels, and house-label lines for one Canadian and five American department store chains. All of our product offers the retailers a premium margin of around Cdn$5 on the lower-priced goods, and Cdn$10 on the higher-priced items against comparable-quality shirts from other manufacturers who own their facilities.

I also get to travel, to work with our contractors and suppliers in China, Pakistan and Panama, and run a Canadian sales force that piggybacks on Sam Spiegel's reps. Benny works with clothing designers in New York for the designs, and runs his own sales staff. We get our materials, all cottons, and findings wherever they're the cheapest, and ship them where needed.

We're profitable. I'm happy, and I don't have to worry about running a plant, or being fired. My biggest concern—mine and Benny's—which is why I travel so much to visit our suppliers, is to ensure the quality control problem doesn't develop again, because we all know that value pricing is valueless if the product isn't of high quality.

. . . .

INTRODUCTION

Retailing is a demanding business under any circumstances, but it is most affected by consumer confidence in the economy and resultant spending patterns. The trend in retailing is towards specialty shops at one end, and huge discount 'mega-stores' and 'category killers', which, between them, are squeezing traditional department store operations—some right out of business.

Consumer sophistication is also increasing. People are demanding more from merchants than just price, value, or service as incentives to do business with them. A trend to watch is loyalty management programs, which offer consumers deeper discounts, or bonuses for restricting their buying to specific businesses, or groups of businesses.

To succeed in retailing, a business must stand out in some way, whether by providing better product, better product knowledge and after-sales service, better pricing, better location or access to a retail operation. Retailers must be finely tuned to the marketplace, and ask themselves: What do I want to sell? Why am I selling it? Does my town/city/community/suburb need another _____?

Retailers must also be able to trigger in people the desire to give them their business, and that might be because of: charm; ambience; perception of the retailer as a kind person, or someone who should be helped, or someone who makes consumers feel better about themselves through association; or the retailer's particular expertise. The retailer must have something to offer the customer which goes beyond the product.

Retailing requires a huge amount of time and energy on the retailer's part. The trend to seven-day-a-week shopping means the retailer must be available to run the retail operation at all times, and to recruit, train and manage effective staff. The greatest challenge facing small retailers is how to meet the time demands of business, and still have a decent personal life.

Also best categorized as retail operations are mail-order businesses, though, like manufacturing operations, they involve little contact with the public, and, like MLM, they significantly reduce the cost of delivery of goods. Mail order is, however, an art, particularly in the matter of managing inventories.

Mail order is a low-overhead delivery system for goods that has been in use for years, primarily as a result of client solicitation through advertisements in various publications. Mail order is poised for even greater market penetration with the rapidly developing technique of product sellers using half-hour TV commercials to demonstrate and pitch their products to the home buyer.

START-UP/CAPITAL INVESTMENT
Retail operations can be bought or started for less than $100,000, depending on location, product lines, and the retailer's ability to negotiate credit from suppliers. There is, however, no limit to what a retailer can spend to get into business. Location, design, construction, fixtures, inventory, business licences, opening promotion/advertising can be quite expensive. Even minimalist warehouse stores must be designed, and need fixtures.

COMPETITIVE ADVANTAGE
Competitive advantage is the retailer's to capture or surrender, depending on his or her ability to offer, and deliver, a better product at a better price, in a superior location.

AUTONOMY OF OPERATIONS
Retailing is a highly autonomous business. The retailer is his or her own boss, needs to be well organized and disciplined, and must have, or quickly acquire, retailing and product expertise.

PAPERWORK BURDEN
Retailers are responsible for administering: federal and provincial income and sales taxes (paid quarterly); annual returns; municipal business licence and business taxes. Retailers who have employees must administer: unemployment insurance; Workers' Compensation;

federal pension plan contributions; employee health plans, and other private insurance plans (if any).

CONTACT WITH PUBLIC
Contact with the public is intense and constant. Retailers open their doors to the public and hope the invitation will be accepted. Retailers must be prepared to have parades of people with a broad range of behavior move through their shops. So, retailers must have high tolerance levels for client behavior, and the skill and tact to establish limits of acceptable behavior from staff and clientele.

INVENTORY REQUIREMENTS
Inventory requirements can be high, to stock the store with an adequate supply of goods to meet the demand the retailer can build. Client goodwill is not generated by disappointing someone who wants to spend some money. A seasoned retailer can learn to manage inventories, especially with an appropriate computer system.

RISK LEVEL
There is a high risk to independent retailing, because it is so dependent on consumer confidence and goodwill, and overall economic conditions. This business requires large front-end cash outlays for location, design, fixtures, inventory, promotion/advertising, operating lines, acquiring and training reliable staff.

FREEDOM OF MOVEMENT OF INDIVIDUAL
A large part of a retailer's life and fortunes are tied in to a shop in a particular location, which requires the retailer's presence there on a regular and consistent basis to protect the investment, and to generate business. One of the most consistent complaints, or worries, expressed by retailers is that the demands of business often interfere with living a decent life. Others who didn't voice the complaint, but were asked about it, suggested that balance comes of recognizing being in business is a part of living, not a substitute for having a life, by setting boundaries between the two, and operating on the principle that killing oneself with work is not a route to success.

. . . .

PAUL ANDREWS: I was one of three environmental protection officers
with a company in Alberta that strip-mined low-sulphur coal for
use in electrical generating plants. The company was controlling
costs by dropping staff levels, and I figured my name would hit the
lay-off lists long before I had a hope of becoming my department's
manager. So, when the company offered a voluntary severance
program, I applied for it.

The company was one of the first sponsors of the Oswego
program, and besides severance pay, counselling and other help, we
were offered a chance to compete for the one spot in the pilot program
reserved for anyone nominated by the company. I got the spot, and
I needed it, because I had a retail business in mind, an ecology shop.
Now it had been a hazy concept when I started thinking about it,
but I clarified my thinking, here, as I wrote my business plan.

You see, the environment has been an important topic of
conversation for years, since the early '70s, but more talk than action
has been focused on it. Oh, people in powerful places, and regular
folk, are concerned, but there's a generational problem in dealing
with environmental issues.

Older politicians and business leaders have to admit the old ways
of doing politics and business don't work any more, but the admission
would also mean admitting they're dinosaurs. Environmentalism as
a mass movement also doesn't seem to work, because it depersonalizes
environmental issues and makes them someone else's problem, when
the key is that each of us has to acknowledge the problem. We're each
part of it, and we're each part of the solution.

Reducing, reusing and recycling is great policy, but it's also
hard to do for individuals brought up on plenty, disposability, and
plenty of disposability. It also happens that there is little in the way
of support for individual environmental responsibility. Think about
it. Where do you go to get the tools and guidance necessary to be
an environmentally friendly human being?

I see there aren't many takers for that question here. That's
understandable. It's 1995, and Earth Tones is still one of a handful

of ecology stores in the country, not much different from 1990, when I was contemplating starting the business.

Researching the product mix was my greatest challenge. I mean, what do you put into an ecology shop? Using the program's facilities, we ran some marketing studies and focus groups, and came up with a mishmash of ideas of what the public wanted—all pretty vaguely stated as help in recycling.

Then I tried another route, and researched the companies manufacturing what we could call ecology products. The range went from high-tech to high-flake. I started sorting out the obvious, like can presses, recycling containers, safe, environmentally friendly soaps and household chemicals, writing supplies, even a small clothing and textiles line.

Then, one day, I ran across an article about an ecology shop in California that geared part of its product line to people with environmental allergies, and I had my moment of inspiration. I researched people with environmental allergies, and found this was a potentially huge, but untapped market. The product selection available to people with allergies is slim, things as basic as water and air purifiers all the way up to hermetically sealed, environmentally safe housing units. They can't really be called a product line, because the production is fragmented, spread among a number of unrelated specialty manufacturers serving niche markets that aren't necessarily allergy oriented, and only merchandised as an 'environmental allergy line' by a few independent sellers like that California shop.

So, I expanded my product mix to include many allergy related goods, though I only stock the smaller pieces and sell the rest through catalogue and agency arrangements with the manufacturers. It's a good working arrangement.

The first year I was in business in Calgary, I drew a modest salary, and the store made a tiny profit. I also found that the work I had done managing teams of people in land reclamation projects had prepared me to serve the public.

I found I like working with people, and they respond well to that attitude. And, if a client becomes an irritant, I use the conflict resolution skills I developed over the years to defuse the situation, or politely invite the client not to come back because his attitude to my staff makes his patronage unwelcome.

It was a risk to turn people away, but I had to learn, and I did it the hard way by tolerating some terribly abusive people who responded to the tolerance by becoming even more abusive, then almost losing my best employee. See, the choice came down to one customer who cost a lot more to serve than his business earned me, or keeping the employee, whose friendly, open nature and excellent service skills ensured the loyalty of 30 clients, and made her a profit centre. It was an important lesson for me—environmentally friendly doesn't only describe how we must treat the environment, but how we must treat each other.

Anyway, the growth in our second year was three times what I projected, because I tried something different. First, I bugged the local papers and TV stations to do stories about us. They didn't until a medical convention of allergists came to town and they did some reports on the conference. Some people they interviewed, some from as far away as the east coast, had heard about my store and came to see it, and it was, indeed, unique. Then the media did some stories on the shop, and one of the reports went national. That raised our profile right across the country, and suddenly people were calling me from all over, asking me to ship them things they couldn't get except with expensive, time-consuming, cross-border mail ordering.

Mail order! For about three weeks I read everything I could get my hands on about mail order and direct marketing. I shaped my plan, then put together a letter, brochure and what I now know was a primitive catalogue, which I then sent to everyone who attended the conference, and all the people who had called after the news piece went national. I also advertised our line of allergy-related goods in three magazines—one business magazine, one lifestyle magazine, and an environmentally focused magazine. The requests came in for catalogues. I sent them out, and, within four weeks, orders were coming in for everything from air purifiers to vegetable-dyed, 100-per-cent cotton clothing for people who can't wear synthetics.

Four months after starting the mail order side of the business, I could no longer service it from the storeroom at my store. So I rented a 500-square-foot shop next to mine, and it was barely adequate for most of the next five months.

Because we were rapidly developing expertise as a mail-order operation, other businesses that needed mail-order work offered to pay us to do their work on contract. Pretty soon, we had to move again to meet our mailing needs, and those of our clients. Here's the checklist for 1995: There are two Earth Tones stores in Calgary, one in Edmonton, and another is opening in Vancouver under a licensing and partnership arrangement with one of my cousins and her husband. We run a profitable mail-order business that services Earth Tones, but is also a profit centre because it services other clients.

Now, I say all this, not because I want to trumpet my successes, but rather that of the program. You see, I made my success, but I was prepared for it because Kevin and the incubator staff encouraged me to break out of the narrow, compartmentalized thinking I had engaged in as a middle-rank line manager for a large corporation. As the boss of my own business, I have to think panoramically, concentrate on a bigger picture, and foster a large-scale business perspective. That's how I saw the allergy aids, mail-order sales, and mail-order servicing as opportunities for me and Earth Tones.

. . . .

TEAM FIVE, SERVICE PROVIDING AND PROFESSIONAL
SERVICES REPORT, OCTOBER 1990
EXECUTIVE SUMMARY

INTRODUCTION
The service business covers a huge constellation of activities. All of these activities, however, have one common characteristic that distinguishes them from the other types of businesses: they provide solutions to problems consumers are unable or unwilling to provide for themselves, that do not always involve a product.

The person who runs an office cleaning business, a sales representative, an independent insurance agent, a writer, corporate trainer, plumber, electrician, computer consultant—these are all examples of service providers.

START-UP/CAPITAL INVESTMENT
Most service and professional services businesses generally require low capital investments. Primary costs are the tools of a particular business: gardening tools, cleaning gear, computer, fax, cellular

phone. Home offices are inexpensive to equip and run. Shared offices with other independents provide a sense of community and split costs. Utilizing office centres can reduce the need for capital outlays on certain equipment and provide the sense of community.

COMPETITIVE ADVANTAGE

Service providers create their competitive advantages. Much depends on the service provider's ability to convince potential clients he or she offers, and can deliver, the best, or, at least, a better service, or solution, at a more attractive or competitive price than any of the competition.

AUTONOMY OF OPERATIONS

This is a business for individualists who like being their own bosses, and enjoy the challenge of learning and using a variety of skills. It requires a defined and marketable expertise, skill or talent, self discipline and strong organizational skills.

PAPERWORK BURDEN

The service provider must take care of general administrative work to keep an office or business going. Primary concerns are managing income and expense records for federal and provincial income and sales tax reporting. Regulations about home-based businesses, which many of these service business often are, vary dramatically across the country, from city to city. Check with local authorities about licensing, zoning, bylaws, and any other regulations of which the service provider should be aware.

CONTACT WITH PUBLIC

Service providing requires high intensity, and constant contact with the public. The service provider is selling services and must always be aware of opportunities to do business with people, and do it. Service providers essentially recruit their clientele, and though some clients find out about service providers by word of mouth, service providers are always marketing their services to potential clients.

INVENTORY REQUIREMENTS

Service providers have low inventory requirements for hard goods, except as needed to provide their services. Otherwise, the service provider's inventory is his or her experience, and ability to get things done.

RISK LEVEL
The risk level is low for service providers, unless the service provided requires expensive equipment.

FREEDOM OF MOVEMENT OF INDIVIDUAL
Service providing is full of highly mobile business opportunities. They could be seasonal, or require extensive travel. Offices outside the home are optional. Tasks can be performed anywhere. The opportunities are limited only by the imagination of the person(s) behind the service.

The potential downside of service businesses is they are usually one-person operations in which revenues are only being generated when the operator is working. This situation could limit opportunities for holidays, time off, personal and family time.

. . . .

FROM THE TRANSCRIPT OF **THE BUSINESS OF CHOICE**, A PANEL DISCUSSION AND WORKSHOP AT THE 1995 OSWEGO COLLEGE SELF-EMPLOYMENT CONFERENCE

KATE PHILLIPS: When Associated Canadian Telephones (ACTEL) closed its Mississauga-based international division in 1988, the axe fell on me, but I wasn't surprised. I was the human resources executive wielding the axe.

I had been part of an in-house task force that found the best way to improve the division's efficiency and productivity was to decentralize and establish offshore sales and service support centres. The cost was 180 jobs at head office, including mine.

I had some regrets about voting my job into oblivion, but I also saw it as an opportunity. But opportunity for what? Did I want another corporate slot? A different work environment? Maybe I could open that boutique I had thought about.

A two-week decompression period on a Martinique beach helped me focus on opportunity. Another corporate job wasn't appealing, and the boutique idea was nice, but unrealistic, because all I know about the retail business is how to shop. No, I'm a human resources professional, and I decided I would do well to stick to what I know. I decided to hang out a consulting shingle. The doing was a plunge into cold waters.

My corporate umbrella was gone. I didn't have a strong business network to tap for work. Making cold calls to potential clients was a lot harder than teaching people how to make the cold calls. And I had no business plan. It was all so overwhelming, because the difference between an entrepreneurial venture and a corporate job is like night and day.

I flailed around quite a bit, lost in my own ignorance. Pure luck got me my first contract, with ACTEL, which contracted with me to do what I had been doing before—training people. That series of contracts, and a few smaller ones I got as referrals, kept me going, but weren't going to make me rich. Then I saw an advertisement about the Oswego program. I examined the outline, and decided this was for me. So I set my sights on a spot in that first class, and I got it.

When we did the business reports, I was on the service business team. I knew I was going to go back to my fledgling training and consulting business when the program was over, and I wanted an inside track on how the business works. I had even kept my ACTEL contracts going during the program, to stay in touch. Anyway, it was in the group that I focused on why I had had a problem in business. I hate cold calling, but business is so competitive, you have to get your name out there in front of people, preferably on a personal basis. And cold calling, just targeting someone and going after an appointment with that someone to ask for business, was so terrifying for me, my teeth would hurt at thought of picking up that phone, and I would freeze before even touching the receiver.

Now Kevin and Kieron and the program instructors had brought in some trainers to work with us on cold calling in simulated situations, and those people worked hard to help those of us who experienced 'call avoidance' get over it. I was particularly stubborn on a subconscious level about that fear, until one day, a trainer looked at me and said, "You dislike rejection. You take it personally, which is unreasonable, especially on a cold call, if the person you're calling doesn't even know you."

Oh, talk about personal revelation. She had something else to say. "The real problem is not the rejection, but, rather, you wanting a positive reaction, a yes, to everything you propose. But life doesn't work that way. There are situations over which you have control, and those over which you don't. You don't have control over someone's response to your phone call. So give it up and just make the phone calls, already, and be your naturally friendly, outgoing, charming self. Let your 'you' shine through, so they want to talk to you more, in person."

Now that's easier said than done. It took me a week to understand what she had said, and when I finally did, I wanted to know why I was so thick I couldn't see it myself. But the key was not to beat myself up for being afraid to call because I feared not getting the response I wanted. So why waste the time? Rather, I began to train myself to believe the call was no different than calling the library and asking for information. Sounds simple, I know, but, then, how many of you heard Kevin say something like, 'The elegant solutions are always the simple ones.'?

I started even before the program ended, calling everyone I thought could use my services, or might know someone who could use my services...and I did it with zest, zeal and dedication. Now, four years later, I operate a prosperous national management training consultancy from my home using a number of contract associates who generate a six figure annual cash flow. My own income is a fair increase over my generous ACTEL salary, and allows me to continue my research into shopping. Earnings aside, though, I am happy, my husband has joined the company to run the administrative side of it, and we're thriving in the entrepreneurial environment of constant change—new projects, new people, managing my own work and career—it's all exciting and enrichening. And best of all, we had our first child last year, a little boy, and at no time have I felt career and motherhood to be a burden the way so many of my friends who are still employed in the corporate world describe it.

There is a critical lesson I have learned as a self-employed service provider that I want to stress, though: Never be embarrassed to ask for money that is due to you.

Never assume that the people you work with, who have regular jobs, understand what drives you, or your business needs, or even care. They work in bureaucratic structures, and get paid every two weeks, whether they produce results or not. Once they've cut a deal with you for work, they figure the bills will get paid...eventually... somehow. They don't understand the importance of having cash flowing effectively. They don't see a problem when an invoice isn't paid in a timely fashion because it's mislaid or ignored. They might talk about the concept, but don't necessarily understand that time has a price, because their time is always paid for.

So, we independents must always be on top of our receivables, always monitoring income, and always paying attention to the critical details of getting paid, and not being embarrassed to push for payment. There are dozens of ways to do that, but I found the most effective is to always find out who is in charge of issuing the cheques, make sure it's okay within the administrative structure of the company I'm dealing with to deal directly with that person on matters of payment, and then establish personal contact. It doesn't always mean I get paid exactly as people agree to pay—bureaucracies have their own habits—but I have few complaints about cash flow problems.

CHAPTER FIVE

Building a Road Map for Success

1990, October: *A Lecture Hall At Oswego College*

"There's only one reason to write a plan: *to get a clear picture in your mind of what you propose to do,*" Mac said confidently. This pleased Kevin. He liked it when he could get one of his students to take over a lecture, and speak from his or her experience. So, when Mac offered to team teach this session, Kevin happily accepted. He was still finding his way around the art of teaching and motivating and keeping the teaching grounded in the experience, rather than the theory of business. So, experimenting was in order, and was proving invaluable, because Kevin was learning the best way to get people to learn something new, or sharpen an old skill, is to get them to teach it.

"The plan is an exercise in logic and ordering information to create a clear, written portrait of how you would go about taking a project to completion," Mac said. "It's like a story. If it's incomplete, you will know, your readers will know, and if your readers are bankers or investors, you'll have trouble raising money on an unclear or incomplete story."

Kevin was fascinated. He always liked meeting people who understood discipline but knew how to keep it from making them rigid and as dangerous as the undisciplined. Mac had kept him wondering those first weeks if he was just an old soldier and cop, set in his ways, seeing the world in absolutes. He had offered little, had kept quiet, absorbed information, and asked a few good, shrewd questions. Occasionally, Mac would drop a clue, maybe intentionally, maybe not. From the clues, Kevin suspected Mac had gained valuable planning experience from his military days, and he wasn't disappointed when Mac showed up with a prepared text based on their conversations of how the class would work, overheads, and copies of an early draft of his business plan to model for his classmates.

Kevin liked learning from his students. It helped him keep a balance between his business role and this teacher thing. Fulfilling the Elmag contract was an easy task that allowed him more than adequate time to teach and keep an eye open for interesting projects to contract to, or invest in. He was already bankrolling a computer programmer as he developed software that would use sound and high-resolution graphics to create computer catalogues for home shoppers, to be distributed by disk, or over cable TV, or telephone lines. Two other projects also looked interesting.

"If the story doesn't work, then there are flaws in the plan, or its underlying assumptions," Mac continued. "The flaws must be addressed, and rectified, or the plan scrapped and redone from the beginning, to create something workable."

Mac is good at this, Kevin thought. He had mentioned that, as an officer in the Forces, he had been required to teach courses. It showed.

"And there's a bonus to having a plan," Mac said. "Should something go wrong, you can take guidance from your plan, and use it to focus on adapting or adjusting it. It can also point you to the way out, so you can prevent a difficult situation from becoming a disaster."

"Now there's the good soldier talking, Mac," Kevin said from where he sat with the students. "You're almost talking life and death situations, and we—" He rose, and indicated the other students, instructors and visitors around the room. "—we just want to run our businesses effectively. But if we build in a way out, aren't we hedging on our commitment, which could stand in the way of success?"

"Being practical is a big part of business and business success," Mac said. "If a business isn't working, you want to know your options to make it work, or to back away and cut your losses."

"True enough," Kevin said. "I know a fellow in marketing analysis with the Federal Business Development Bank who's burning out on reading plans and loan requests from manufacturers looking for financing who are actually out of business, but don't know it, or refuse to recognize it."

"So it helps to have a fallback or bailout position, because no matter how good your research, training, analysis, or any other preparation, you'll still generally base most of your decisions on informed guesswork," Mac said. "It could happen that you encounter conditions you can't control or manage, or something that invalidates your assumptions."

"I like that, Mac," Kevin said. "Use your plan to explore alternatives. Keep in mind there are alternatives, know how to use them, and how you can cut losses in a bad situation."

"Makes sense," Mac shrugged. "If you have a limited set of resources and they're badly deployed—"

"Mac, let's substitute money or investment for resources," Kevin suggested.

Mac's expression showed he wasn't quite sure what Kevin meant.

"Okay, let's say you earmark $50,000 to start a security business, and you target banks as your primary client market. You also market yourself as a security consultant to retail stores like The Grange, which have asked you to provide staff training seminars, and—"

"Nice idea," Mac said, and wrote some notes on his papers.

"—you find that though you're an experienced hand at bank-related security issues, you've come up against a bit of market resistance you didn't anticipate, because no one suggested it might be a factor. Assume the banking community now treats you as an outsider, and is so paranoid it will only work with official crime prevention agencies and in-house security people. What do you do?"

"Well, if achieving my strategic target is immediately unattainable, I would keep up my momentum by focusing on the target of opportunity—"

"Uh, Mac, what do you mean by target of opportunity?" Brenda asked.

"Well, you have two types of target, the one that you have defined as your goal, the one that must be achieved for you to claim success. That's the strategic target," Mac said. "The target of opportunity is an attractive opportunity that presents itself as you're working towards achieving the strategic target, and can be exploited without deflecting you from, or dissipating the energy you can direct towards the strategic target."

"They're like little unexpected gifts," Brenda chuckled.

Mac grinned and nodded. "Use them all you can. The security seminars are just that; I hadn't thought of them as an opportunity until Kevin mentioned them. Now, I see a whole division devoted to business and personal security seminars."

"Think of women as a big market for the personal security seminars," Brenda suggested.

"Done," Mac nodded as he scribbled more notes to himself. "I would exploit the opportunity presented by the seminars and use them to ensure I had a sound business and financial base to work from to penetrate other markets," Mac said. "Concurrently, I would continue developing what had been my strategic target— the bank security business."

"That's why a good plan has to offer flexibility," Kevin said to the class.

Mac nodded. "It just shows the direction you're going, and how you're going to get there, and highlights potential detours and such, as you'll see when we go through a planning process."

"Being open to the target of opportunity is a critical issue, everyone," Kevin said. "It can sometimes become a whole business, which is what happened to Daniel Best, who owns a company called AirCare Products. He dressed up one of the annual managers' meetings of A Chip Off The Old Block, when I was its president..."

Daniel had had a succession of tedious jobs between leaving high school in 1968 and going to work in Toronto's theatre world as a technician, then stage manager, and finally a production manager. From there, he moved on to production management for industrial shows, consulting to production designers, even designing and building presentation theatres for corporations. His plan had always been the same, to do what he loved: play with gadgets and special effects and get paid to do it.

He and his wife, Amy, worked together to establish their financial goals and the like, and generally, everything worked out. The work was lucrative, and they met their targets, sometimes exceeding them, but by the mid-'80s, Daniel was becoming dissatisfied and bored with the amount of time he was spending on the road, away from home, away from Amy and their young daughter Isobel.

"Then, on a trip to the U.S., I saw this confetti cannon," Daniel said one day when Kevin visited his office to work out the show for the 1987 managers' meeting. Daniel gestured wildly as he described the workings of a long plastic tube, with a valve and carbon dioxide cylinder attached to one end, which is filled with tamped-down confetti. "A trigger mechanism releases a blast of CO_2, and BOOM!, confetti blows out in a shower that can cover a room. I figured this was it—" Daniel almost growled out the words. "—the product that would let me do what I want to do without the travel. I would just get the rights for Canada and sell the cannon to everyone."

He contacted the creator of the cannon and arranged an exclusive deal for eastern Canada. He had an idea of how large the 'event' market was, because he was already servicing it, but Daniel did more research into the business, figured out the approach he would take and wrote his plan to sell the hell out of the confetti cannon. He formed his new company AirCare Products as the business vehicle, and created a brochure about the cannon and the company. He put together a list of potential clients, sent them the brochure, then followed up with phone calls. *He was devastated to learn no one wanted to buy the cannon.*

"But they asked, 'What else do you have, and what other services do you provide?', and I said, 'What do you need?'" Daniel laughed. "The cannon opened the doors to commercialize other things I had done on a small scale over the years in theatre and for industrials." That included indoor pyrotechnics and special effects, a fairly wide open market for audiences jaded by television, but still awed by things that go bang, pop, whizz and whistle, safely, indoors.

AirCare Products quickly went from being a cannon distribution company to a pyrotechnics and special effects company. Daniel, nicknamed The Pyro Guy by his daughter, now designs and performs effects for clients, and rents gear and equipment he imports, or custom builds himself, to other special effects people. He's begun developing a sophisticated line of electronically triggered effects that increase the 'aah' quotient of his shows, and overall, he's having a great time, happily blowing things up and entertaining people. Oh, and the confetti cannon? People prefer to rent them...often.

"So, be open to the target of opportunity—you never know when it will appear. Write something about being prepared for it, as a reminder, into your plan," Kevin urged his audience. "And there you have my view on the business plan: It's an analytical and organizational tool that keeps you focused on success."

Mac nodded. "You can use it to keep you from panicking and running off out of control, making unsound judgements. Half the battle of dealing with disaster, or any other challenging situation, is not panicking."

"So, the plan is a clear picture of your vision, where you're going, how you're going to get there, the cost to get there, and the payoffs," Kevin said. "It's the step to take now that you've shaped a world-view, done your personal inventory, defined your goals, and determined the kind of business structure that best serves your needs, and works to your strengths."

Kevin sat down and Mac took over the class again. "A plan isn't a tool to use only when starting a business," he said, putting a transparency on the overhead projector and covering it before switching on the machine. Only the title of the sheet showed, but, as Mac spoke, he uncovered the transparency line by line, and read its contents.

WHEN TO CREATE OR REVISE A PLAN

Create a plan when you intend to do anything major in a business like:

1. Start your business;
2. Expand;
3. Develop new products or services;
4. Make major operating or management decisions;
5. Take new business directions;
6. Recapture control of a situation gone awry; or
7. Seek outside financing or investment.

Mac read through the list one more time when it was fully exposed, then walked away from the projector, closer to his listeners. "Now, as to the features or characteristics of a plan..."

. . . .

FROM THE TRANSCRIPT OF **THE BUSINESS PLAN**, A WORKSHOP AT THE 1995 OSWEGO COLLEGE SELF-EMPLOYMENT CONFERENCE *(Available from Allied Tape and Transcription Services Ltd., c/o Oswego College, $8.50 a copy, sales taxes included.)*

ANNE PORTER: Most of the first two months in the program, I just kept my mouth shut. I was a secretary, or at least that had been my last job, before I was 'horizontally sliced' from the Consolidated Steel Company of Canada. Horizontally sliced is how the management consultants described a form of downsizing that involved cutting out the entire 12th floor of management. Funny thing is, nobody I know who worked on the 11th or 13th floors ever missed us.

I started there as a clerk-typist when I left high school in 1980, and I took secretarial courses in night school. I had made it to executive secretary, assigned to a middle manager, when the lights went out in '88 on 12, at CSC headquarters in downtown Toronto. I worked for a while as an office temporary so I could take more courses, because I really didn't want to become an old secretary. I was thinking of setting up a temp service for people trained and skilled in particular computer programs and applications, but I knew nothing about setting up or running a business. I had heard about the Oswego program, and was able to get into that first class, what people have taken to calling 'The 20'.

I had always thought of a business plan as nothing more than a money-raising tool, because I had typed enough of them as pitches middle managers were making for pet projects. Mind you, I didn't feel bad about it, because most of the people in the class didn't know about them either, except Mac, and Brenda, and she was an accountant. Now I use a business plan as a matter of habit to organize my research, to order information, and analyze how feasible my ideas are.

I mean we had this preamble of Mac and Kevin discussing the plan, and how it could be used, and well, it was like someone had turned on a light bulb. Then Mac put one of his transparencies on the overhead projector and showed us his list of the seven critical issues that must be addressed when a person is shaping a plan, and it was like the dimmer was turned up to bright.

His list read:

CRITICAL QUESTIONS TO ADDRESS WHEN SHAPING A PLAN
1. What's going on in the marketplace?
2. Does this represent an opportunity for a new business?
3. What is the potential payoff?
4. What am I going to do about it?
5. How am I going to do it?
6. What resources (persons, things, finances) do I have on call, and what additional resources do I need to gather to effectively accomplish what I'm going to do?
7. What other information, research, contacts, or other data do I need to complete the mission?

Mac said there was no 'standard' business plan format, and joked that if it did exist it could be found in Kevin's non-existent National Business League rule book. But he did say formats were available in any number of books on the shelves in bookstores, and they all ask for answers to the same seven big questions in varying degrees of detail. Most chartered banks also have commercial lending units that have prepared outlines and workbooks and other materials to guide new businesspeople, and the Federal Business Development Bank sells guides and business plan development packages for nominal sums. Kevin said there were even computer programs on the market that are templates for business plans. You just have to fill in the information as the program guides you through the process.

Mac mentioned we could get consultants to write our plans, though neither he nor Kevin thought hiring someone to do it for us was a productive alternative. A consultant can produce a professional package, but it still means we haven't sat down, and, with our own time, energy, and effort, thought out our own proposed business.

Then Kevin got on his 'truth in advertising' soapbox to explain why he doesn't believe in having surrogates write your plan, especially the people who use formulas touted as 'winning business plans that raise money from investors'. "They're full of bells and whistles, buzzphrases and cliches that investors and promoters like to hear, but which border on misrepresentation," he said.

So, I got the message loud and clear. We all did. Write your own plan, for yourself, and ensure it makes sense to you and your advisors (lawyer, accountant, etc.), and it covers all the informational territory a good business plan must encompass. Whatever you do, make it ring with *your analysis, your clarity, your truth*. If you need to attract funding, then work with a consultant to add the information that describes the investment you're looking for, and all the extra material investors or bankers need to decide if you're a tolerable investment or lending risk.

. . . .

1990, October: *The Lecture Hall, Oswego College*

"I use a planning method I was taught as a young soldier," Mac said. "It's as good as any used in business."

"Did you know that the business plan as we understand it, as a critical component of business organization, is only about 45 years old?" Kevin interrupted as he looked around the classroom expectantly, waiting for someone to comment. He just got people shaking their heads.

"Well, it's become part of the gospel of business, and it's a good idea...as long as it isn't a straitjacket," he said. "The story I've pieced together from business historians and books is that the generation of business school graduates from the late 1930s, who were drafted into the U.S. Army and put to work running the logistics and administration for World War Two, used its business training within the framework of the military planning system..."

These men saw how effective formal, large-scale, long-term logistical and administrative planning was. When they returned to civilian life after the war, they brought their military-management experience to business life, and provided the administrative expertise to create some of the huge corporations that dominated North America's post-war business right into the '80s. One of the most influential teachers of these wizards was Georges Doriot, a Frenchman teaching at the Harvard Business School, who was asked by the U.S. Army to come to Washington to manage mobilization of America's industries to supply the war effort. He was commissioned a General, so he had the clout to do the job.

"And one of his post-war students, who taught in the management faculty at a community college in Calgary, told me Doriot's text for his class on leadership was a U.S. Army World War Two field manual for officers," Kevin continued. "Now understand, like Mac, I'm not recommending you all march off and enlist. I think that right here we're running the closest thing to a business boot camp you need to start your own businesses. What I really want to stress is the importance to your success of looking at things with the critical eye a plan guides you to see with. Got that?" He looked for confirmation from the class, and was satisfied with the response.

"Okay, Mac, please, walk us through the process," Kevin said.

"Any time I'm faced with a problem, a proposal, or a potential opportunity, I automatically order and process the seven critical planning questions I gave you earlier, in the organizational framework you see here," Mac said as he put up an overhead that read:

PROCESSING INFORMATION FOR A PLAN

1. SITUATION
   a. What's going on in the marketplace?
   b. Does this represent an opportunity for a new business?
2. MISSION
   What am I going to do about it?
3. EXECUTION
   How am I going to do it?
4. SERVICE & SUPPORT
   a. What resources (persons, things, finances) do I have on call, and what additional resources do I need to gather to effectively accomplish what I'm going to do?
   b. What's the potential payoff?
5. CO-ORDINATION
   What other information, research, contacts, or other data do I need to complete the mission?

"In the army, we called number five communications, because it involved those bits of information like radio frequencies, passwords, code name and the like to co-ordinate movement of neighboring units, so we weren't running all over each other," Mac said. "But, for businesses purposes, I changed it to co-ordination, so we have a place to put background information."

He looked around. "Any questions about this processing method?" There were none. "I'm not saying you have to use this particular framework. It works for me. It's easy to work with, and is flexible enough to meet almost any situation." He removed the overhead sheet and replaced it with another he again covered with a sheet of paper. "When you apply this framework to a business plan, it becomes an outline for a detailed document, as you'll see in the next few slides." He removed the paper...

. . . .

ANNE PORTER: After going through their presentation on the background to planning, Mac and Kevin walked us through the process by discussing the items on Mac's overhead. Then, using the framework, we got to do our own, and boy, was that an interesting experience. It was demanding.

There we were, given a classroom exercise, to begin developing our own business plans, and we quickly discovered just how much of our ideas were wishful thinking. I mean, I was sure I had thought out my business idea... Well, just come with me for a little walk through the handout you were given at the start of this session. It's a printout of the computer file I wrote that day. It started as notes from the class on business plans, and followed the template Kevin and Mac gave us, with their comments on each element. Then, I went back through the file, and filled in the template the best I could, with the notes as my guide. Where I couldn't complete a section, I wrote in questions to myself, or points to cover, as I gathered my detailed research. My stuff is in italics.

The drafts that followed this were more detailed, and sophisticated. I present this as the place we start in planning— organizing our first thoughts to bring order to the wishing, test our ideas and assumptions, and get a measure of just how much more we have to find out.

HANDOUT
From Anne Porter's Computer File:
C:\OSWEGO\BIZPLAN\LECNOTES.DOC 30 OCTOBER 1990
Mac and Kevin's Business Plan Template
With notes for DRAFT ONE of Anne Porter's Business Plan

TITLE PAGE
This page should carry:
- name of the company, and a description of the document.
- contact person's name, title, address, phone and fax numbers
- notes about confidentiality, copyright, trademarks, and revision dates.

SKILLS ON DEMAND
Business Plan For A Specialized Skills Office Temporary Service
Prepared by Anne Porter, President
22 Rue Morgue Avenue
Downsview, Ontario M5W 1M7
(905) 555-5000 Fax (905) 555-5500
Draft One, 29 October 1990

PURPOSE AND MISSION PAGE
Present a tightly worded statement of the plan's purpose, and the company's reason for being—the mission statement. Be precise and clear about the topic, and write in the present tense.

INTRODUCTION—THE SITUATION
Corporate downsizings have created short-term demands for individuals trained and experienced in specialized computer applications who can quickly take up a task and execute it cost-effectively. This demand has created the opportunity for a profitable service business focused on matching the appropriate temporaries with the clients.

THE COMPANY AND ITS MISSION
Skills On Demand is in business to provide a high degree of effective service and client satisfaction by matching people with specialized office and computer skills with businesses that need those skills for short-term tasks.

Secondary Mission
The secondary mission is to compile a database of individuals with specialized office skills who seek long-term, regular employment, and match them with clients looking for full-time office staff.

Targets of Opportunity
- Grand strategy establishes the global picture and intentions.
- Strategy defines targets and how to achieve them; defined targets are strategic targets.
- Tactics are the methods by which a strategy is executed.
- Targets of opportunity are opportunities that haven't been defined as strategic targets, but often present themselves in the course of business. If they are beneficial, that is they can

be exploited without diverting time, energy or resources from the strategic drive, they can be pure, low-cost profit. (Kevin reminded us of The Pyro Guy, who started his company as a confetti cannon business, but discovered the real market was in providing indoor pyrotechnics and special effects. So, write in a paragraph that gives an idea how I'm going to deal with targets of opportunity.)

Skills On Demand will remain open to opportunities to meet developing needs in the office staffing industry, and will capitalize upon these opportunities where they offer the potential of profit. An example is roving computer operators for businesses that share offices, or in office centres.

TABLE OF CONTENTS

EXECUTIVE SUMMARY
This is the part of the document an outside investor, or banker, reads first. Usually a page or two, rarely as many as four; any longer and you're writing the plan itself.

THE CONCEPT
Describes the business.

Skills On Demand is a company positioned to serve specific needs in the office temporary staffing business, particularly for people with specialized skills and experience on particular office machines or computer applications. Skills On Demand differentiates itself from other office temporary services because it matches people to specific tasks, rather than just sending out office temporaries to fill in for a while. This ensures the temporaries can give maximum cost-effectiveness to clients. To this end, Skills On Demand staff work closely with clients and service providers to ensure efficient and effective matches to meet demands.

BUSINESS BACKGROUND
- Briefly list the reasons the opportunity exists.
- Present the business potential, in dollars and market size.
- Summarize how the company will gain access to the market. How, specifically, will this company participate? Directly? Through agents? Distributors? Partnerships?

QUESTIONS TO ANSWER: Size of the temp industry in Toronto? The number of competitors? Any with my focus? Best way to penetrate market?

SUCCESSFUL MODELS

Briefly note similar ventures, how they work, and how your business is different.

There was time when all office skills were common in content and execution. Typing, bookkeeping, financial recording and reporting could all be handled by people with similar skills in offices which had little variation in equipment or technology. In short, anyone with typing skills could type on any typewriter.

Today, there is a huge array of computer programs, each with its own operating style, and little standardization from office to office. The temp who can operate five word-processing programs in two operating systems with equal efficiency is a rarity. Individuals with experience in specific programs on specific platforms aren't rare, but they are in demand as temps when staff office workers are ill, on maternity leave, or, for some reason, must take protracted leaves without quitting. It is more efficient to engage a temp with specific skills who can immediately go to work, rather than someone who has to undergo a learning curve on the company's equipment and software.

POINTS TO ADD: Get a list of temps. Note the chains and stand-alones. Name some of the services. Describe their workings—they match bodies to empty slots and are more concerned with processing numbers of people than in matching skills. Any like mine?

FUNDING REQUIRED

A brief statement of the capital needed to create the company and move it to profitability, the time frame for spending the money, and how funds will be spent, i.e. offices, inventory, project development.

POINTS TO COVER: I would need an income to run the business while recruiting the temps and building a client data and contact base. Office costs. Furniture. Phones. Office services. Maybe I should look into renting space in a business centre until I can justify setting up my own offices. What about a home office and an outside

answering service? Third option: Operate out of a briefcase with a
cellular phone and laptop computer. Better get numbers and build
comparison budgets.

REWARDS TO THE COMPANY
A brief projection of the scale, nature, and timing of payback to
the company on expenditures.
POINTS TO COVER: Depends on budget.

REWARDS TO INVESTORS (if applicable)
A brief projection of the scale, nature, and timing of return on
investment, to investors, or payback schedules for lenders, which
includes tax benefits, if any, for investors.
POINTS TO COVER: Depends on budget.

SUMMARY
Recap the concept and rewards, and sum up with a statement
like: We believe what we propose is an excellent, feasible and
profitable venture. We are looking for investors interested in
long-term profit potential.
POINT: This has to wait until the overall plan is complete.

THE PLAN—NEW PAGE
SITUATION
This establishes that an opportunity exists to create a profitable
business. If information is available, this section mentions the type
and size of the market potential in terms of geography, finances, and
demographics. Present the information in strong, simple, declarative
sentences. Think of this as the premise of your argument.

Corporate downsizings have created short-term demands for
individuals trained and experienced in specialized computer applica-
tions. This demand has created the opportunity for a profitable
service business focused on matching the appropriate temporaries
with clients.

The primary market targeted for Skills On Demand is small busi-
nesses of up to 50 employees. There are (find out how many)
companies of this size in the Toronto region, which represent the
market to be developed.

POINT TO COVER: It doesn't look like I can put a $ figure on what I think the market represents, so I should consider setting income targets.

INDUSTRY BACKGROUND
This provides additional information about the industry, and how it runs, in terms accessible to someone who isn't of the industry.

Traditionally, temp service agencies develop databases of temporary service providers, develop contact lists, and have salespeople who market the service. The agencies either earn commissions on the temps' wages, or charge clients flat rate service fees. When a client calls in a requisition, a temp is dispatched. Rarely is the temp matched to specific client applications and needs, because most agencies are just concerned with filling orders. The service becomes a hit-and-miss arrangement that might or might not meet the needs of all involved.

So, as needs have become more specialized, and productivity has become more important in business, temps who can move directly into tasks and complete them with minimal time loss could be in high demand. The key is having an agency that can match the temps with client needs.

ORGANIZING FOR SUCCESS
This is a list of the components necessary to create an entity focused on success.

To succeed, this business needs adequate financing (see budgets), management, information, and sales and marketing resources to sustain operations so an appropriate and diversified list of temps can be recruited, a client base can be developed, and the 'matchmaking' can begin, so revenues can be generated.

STRATEGIC FOCUS
Establish short-term (one- to two-year), mid-term (two- to four-year), and long-term (four years and 'as far ahead as you want to push it') visions for the company.
–   The long-term vision illustrates the big picture, what you want your company to become. Short and mid-term visions describe the steps to achieving the long-term vision.

–   Be realistic, keep the objective in mind, and outline the steps
    to achieve the objective.

*Management's long-term focus is on developing and holding
enough of the potential market share for temp services among companies in the London to Ottawa corridor to generate $2 million gross
income per year for the company by its fifth year of operations.*

*The short-term goal is to generate $125,000 of gross income
for the company in its first year of operations. The mid-term goal is
to double that growth each year until the long-term goal has been
reached.*

*POINT TO PONDER: Is this realistic? Can I get up and running quickly
enough to generate those first-year earnings? Rethink!*

THE COMPANY AND ITS MISSION

*Information for this section is the same as that in the executive
summary.*

The statement of purpose.

SECONDARY MISSION

TARGETS OF OPPORTUNITY

ORGANIZATION OF THE COMPANY

Define organizational and business philosophy, and company
structure, i.e. stay small, keep overhead low, use only sub-
contractors, just-in-time delivery arrangements with suppliers, or
grow large, dominate the market, occupy floor 12 somewhere.

OPERATIONS

Detail how the company will conduct business.

*POINTS TO COVER: Come back to this section after I've researched
and constructed comparison budgets for operating from an office
suite, a business centre, home, from a briefcase.*

OPERATIONAL PRIORITIES

This section establishes the precedence of execution of the short-,
mid- and long-term strategies.

*The company's operators will work towards the goals as defined
in the strategic focus section as follows:*

1. *Work towards short-term goals to generate a personal income
    and business revenues.*

2.   *While working to meet mid-term growth goals.*
3.   *While working to meet long-term market-share and revenue goals.*

EXECUTION

This is the tactical plan. It shows how the strategy or strategies will be executed, by breaking the big picture down into the tasks necessary to complete the plan. Tasks must be treated as consecutive (a series of activities), or concurrent (performed parallel to each other), or a mix of both.

POINTS TO CONSIDER: I have to think this part through a bit further. I have to decide if I'm going to manage and act as a temp in the first year, or just manage. That choice will affect my decision about what is the most effective way to do business, in terms of offices and mobility. The decision on managing only, or managing and being a temp, too, affects the pace at which I can work to the short-, mid-, and long-term goals. (This is like putting together a jigsaw puzzle for which I'm manufacturing each piece as I place it.)

OPERATIONAL TARGETS

Generally established as time targets, with tasks defined as consecutive or concurrent activities, arranged in the necessary sequences. For example, business development—establishing the contacts and credibility to develop the market into which you will be selling—will have to be an ongoing activity run concurrent with client servicing.

—   Example quoted was to set up the first part of the section as client base development. Mac illustrated with an example from his plan:

Targets for Year One:

Recruit a talent pool of 100 individuals. Develop a 400-name potential client list. Acquire 50 active clients.

POINT TO CONSIDER: How do I generate $125,000 in revenues from 50 clients? Rethink goals/assumptions?

Targets for Year Two:

(Be brave, Anne!)

Build the talent list to 250 individuals. Build the potential client list to 800 names. Acquire 100 new active clients.

In Mac's example, he had targets for years three, four and five. Kevin told us not to feel foolish about what might seem extravagant projections, because it's easier to hit targets you're aiming for, rather than those you have a vague idea exist and hope to grab if you can find them.

– Target the people with whom you must establish business relationships.

– Write this into the plan, so you're always ready when someone you didn't expect to get to see for a while shows up. Then you're ready to collar him or her and make that important contact.

– This section should also detail those industry functions such as trade shows, conferences, courses you or your representatives would have to attend on a consistent basis to establish contact networks, profile and credibility, and to stay current on products and techniques in your industry.

– No matter what business you get into, there's a trade association, and, usually, regular trade shows that are invaluable forums for making contacts. *N.B. be careful and target the ones where people actually mix, and you can contact those people you're looking for.

POINTS TO CONSIDER: Check out industry functions, industry movers. (Do they exist?) Define who can help me, figure out how to convince them it's in their interests to help me, then get them to help me.

SERVICES AND SUPPORT

– This section deals with resources that need to be allocated to the business, and analysis of what's on hand, and what needs to be acquired.

POINTS TO CONSIDER: I have skills, but little money. I will have training, but no management experience when the program ends. I know there's a large pool of talent out there, because I work through a temp service. And I know there's demand, because of what I face every time I go out on a job. Stats to back up assumptions?

DEVELOPMENT EXPENSES

This section, or one similarly titled, details the money required to start up the company, and projections of earnings targets. It's usually broken into two sections, the first being a pair of tables that detail:

1. DEVELOPMENT EXPENSES for the development period detailed in the plan, and covering all the projected costs of doing business; and

POINTS TO CONSIDER: Must plan for the first year as that's the critical development year, building talent pool, client lists, contacts— all cash outlay; even if there's income it could be an expensive year. Need start-up money. Consider as potential sources family, friends, government business development programs. Former employers? Why not? Banks? Accch!

Maybe revising the earnings and market share targets by a year—$2 million by year six—is in order.

2. CASH-FLOW PROJECTIONS detail from where you expect to derive income, and when it comes to the company.

The second section can include NOTES ACCOMPANYING DEVEL-OPMENT EXPENSES, and NOTES ACCOMPANYING CASH FLOW EXPENSES, that explain any strange entry or category titles, and generally provide a prose explanation of anything in the tables the planner/writer feels needs clarifying.

PRINCIPALS IN THE COMPANY

The details in this section are simply who's organizing and running the business.

– These details are placed in different sections in different plan formats. Mac places them here because, in this era of knowl-edge work, individual players and their skills and knowledge are business resources, assets to be deployed to achieve the business goals. So, they belong in the service and support section.

Skills On Demand creator and president Anne Porter, 29, has had eight years of experience in office services and management with a major Canadian resources company, and two years experi-ence as an office temporary. She is a graduate (fingers crossed) of the Oswego College Entrepreneurship Incubator.

POINT TO CONSIDER: Pretty thin stuff. I'd best ask around and see what the instructors say about dressing it up.

CO-ORDINATION

Use this section to put in industry research, like heavy statistical data, abstracts of reports, appendices, and information that doesn't fit into the specific sections or subsections that came before, but is important to completing the picture of the company.

POINT TO CONSIDER: This is where I would put my appendices and supporting documents—like a report from the Canadian Federation of Independent Business on the trend to using more office temps, if such a report existed, and I used it—and other external information I used to build the plan that would distract the reader while he/she is going through the plan, but is still important and should be seen, or at least available if anyone besides me is interested...the heavier data.

ANNE PORTER: That's as far as I got that first day. As I say, it was an eye opener. I saw how little I actually knew. It took me another month of research to flesh out the document, because I had to search through library files, deal with people in government research offices who weren't sure what I was talking about. I just spoke slowly, and clearly, in short sentences, and eventually they understood.

I worked on that document well into the second term of the program, then I started implementing it, even before the program was over. I started by recruiting the talent pool. I also decided to operate from an office centre, where I was able to rent a large furnished office with two phone lines, and get office services for about $500 per month. I also took a big chance and hired a salesperson right away, so I was selling half the time and managing the other half.

Understand, I had gathered what to me was a sizeable start-up fund. I put up $7,500 from my own savings, which my two brothers matched. That qualified me for a matching-dollar small business development loan from the provincial government. I also found a pair of guardian angels, who required me to keep them anonymous as a condition of kicking in another $30,000.

We worked hard that first year, and earned enough that we didn't have to spend all of the start-up money. I also had a $25,000 pre-tax profit, and another $15,000 I had put away during the year in company-held GICs and Treasury bills. So, I repaid the provincial loan that first year, which meant I could start paying my brothers and the investors back in Year Two, a year earlier than I anticipated.

I also profit-shared $7,500 to myself, and another to my salesperson, who asked if she could turn it into an investment in the company. I was pleased to let her do that, and she's now a minority shareholder, along with my brothers, while my unnamed guardian angels and I own and control, between us, 75 per cent of the company.

I know, that's brilliant performance for a start-up year. It's also rare, but I realize now I was so naive and terrified of messing up that all of my income projections were extremely conservative. I thought my cash flow would all be out for the first year while I built my talent and client databases. Well, in the first three months, after word of what I was doing got out, I was swamped with resumes, phone calls, and people at my door asking for interviews. As I sorted them out, my salesperson went from a standing start to running full out. Then one day, the phone callers changed from being people looking for work to people looking for workers. Six months later, my accountant called me to tell me I was a success. It was two days before I was able to slow down and realize what she meant. I had been in a profit position as of week two of month seven.

You see, I hadn't considered that the conservatism and fear of company managements in restructuring would work for me. They were cutting costs by cutting staff, but were also getting rid of key support people, thinking they could do without them, which they could, but only part of the time. So, they started using temps on a regular part-time basis to bolster their support work force. And because of our focus in matching skills with needs, rather than filling spaces, we were kept busy filling in their staffing gaps.

The trend continued, and hasn't stopped. Now, in year four, Skills On Demand occupies a suite of offices large enough to house six sales reps and support staff, and we need to expand again to meet demand. We have a talent pool of 500 men and women with management, administration and office skills who just meet our need for skilled bodies to fill the demands made on us for temps. And my accountant projects the company's gross income—not our billings, but our gross income—will likely top $1.75 million.

I attribute the success to date to having a good idea, a quality product and service, marketing them aggressively, and having a good, sensible and *flexible*—let me stress flexible—plan to execute the idea.

Why do I stress flexibility? Because, when I wrote the plan, I didn't anticipate my second largest single potential market, even though it was sitting right under my nose. You, the independent operators, who can't afford or don't want full-time office help. You do need office help on a part-time basis, and I had no trouble adjusting my operations to meet your needs, because I had a plan to work with. So, thank you, and thank you to The Oswego Program, and to Mac and Kevin for teaching me how to build and use a business plan.

. . . .

1990: *The Lecture Hall*

"Once you've completed the plan to the co-ordination section, you have something that is purely an organizational, analytical, and operational document," Mac said. "If, however, you were preparing the plan for potential investors, or to get bank financing, you would then add a section of information covering the details of the investment." Mac turned to Kevin. "And that's where my presentation ends. Kevin..."

"Thanks, Mac," Kevin said as they switched places and Mac joined the rest of the class.

"You'll be dealing with the information needed for investors in a session with one of your finance instructors, because this is the hardest part of a plan for us to discuss in general terms," Kevin said. "If you incorporate and look for private investors, then you have to check with the securities regulators in your province of operations, because each province has its own regulations. If you're looking for bank financing, you'll find each bank has its pet formula for the investment section of the plan."

"So, what's the point of the finance session?" John Tan asked.

"To introduce you to the concepts," Kevin said. "Your best bet, though, is to get help with your offering financials from an experienced accountant or consultant."

"So what do we do, call up a consultant and say, 'Hey, do you know how to write the financials part of a business plan to raise money?'" John asked.

"Well, yes, actually," Kevin said with a laugh. "But I think the best thing to do is ask your lawyer or accountant if he or she can do it, or give you a reference."

"Just the thought of trying to raise money makes me sick to my stomach," Anne Porter called out.

"Naah, it gets easy after the fourth or fifth try," Kevin said. "But don't talk about trying. Trying isn't doing."

"No, it isn't the asking for money that worries me. It's getting it," Anne said to her classmates' laughter.

"Hang on, what Anne says sounds funny, but it's true," Kevin said. "Once you get the money, you have to perform as you promised."

"So what's the successful technique?" Brenda asked.

"Be your own committed, eager-to-win-and-make-people-rich, passionate-to-win-with-your-idea self," Kevin said.

"Well, geez, I can do passion," John interjected. "I can bypass the whole planning part."

"I don't think so, John," Kevin said slowly. "You can never predict what will happen, and how people will respond. I know this geologist…"

Harry Legg started his own mining company after some frustrating experiences while working for large mining firms. He left his job in Toronto in 1984 to buy and exploit a New Brunswick nickel, zinc and silver mine that was unprofitable for one of the majors to run because of its high overheads, but was perfect for a low-cost independent. So, he set about raising the money he needed. He created the company, wrote the business plan, and went through the securities regulations with his accountant. Using his plan as the foundation, he built an offering memorandum he distributed to his target investors.

After pitching one rather cranky potential investor, Harry was sure this was one person with whom he hadn't connected. A few days later, the investor called. "He told me I was crazy, and he was crazy to consider even investing in my company," Harry once told Kevin. "Then he said, 'But I like you, and I think you'll do well. So I'll buy into your crazy scheme anyway.'"

Kevin shrugged. "You never can tell what's going to happen. You control how effectively you pitch, but have no control over the final decision." He started putting his papers into his briefcase, then stopped.

"You know, I heard a flip side to that story from a professional investor I met when I was doing my time in Calgary in the late '70s," Kevin said. "Now the context here is that the business environment in Calgary was heated, in full boom, and the oil industry was rich, running on inflationary steam and expectations. Profits from big oil fuelled construction booms, land speculation booms, feature film booms, and just about any dream a person could conjure out of a pipe..."

The smell of wealth was as strong as the smell of crude oil, and it seemed like every person connected in even the remotest fashion to the oil industry strutted like some wildcatter. The big fantasy in town was, 'I'm smart enough to be my own boss and make a fortune. I want to be my own boss. I'm going into business for myself.'

Kevin had made a presentation on computerization at a Chamber of Commerce luncheon, and a member of the audience had asked him to come by and talk about computerizing his operation. The business turned out to be too specialized and small to justify the cost of a complete mainframe—those were the days before desktop computers—so Kevin set the client's company up in a time-share arrangement with someone else he knew who was happy to rent out excess capacity on a mainframe computer.

The client himself, was, however, a fascinating portrait, and he gave Kevin an important piece of advice about the world of investment. Given to favoring pricey cigars bought one at a time from tony tobacco shops to ensure freshness, and custom-tailored suits of imported fabrics, he had assembled a $10-million capital pool from business associates and friends, and had made big money for those people through shrewd investing. He had a great track record, because most of his investments were in junior and middle-sized oil companies, though, in the mid-'70s, even a blind pig who owned or invested in an oil company couldn't help but make money.

But this investor also had a gambler's streak, sharklike instincts, and a certain degree of *noblesse oblige*. He was 'attitude' writ large about being a player, and winning, and succeeding, and he was in a position to dispense largesse like some feudal lord, which tickled his ego, he freely admitted. He loved the idea of and the kick he got from investing a portion of the capital pool in small companies poised for explosive growth. (For all his lofty reasoning, he also took huge chunks of equity in the high-risk companies, and the investment seekers repaid handsomely for his attentions.)

"I don't invest in businesses," he declared to Kevin. "I invest in people."

"So, how do you decide?" Kevin asked.

"Well, I look at the business plans, and the cash flow projections and all the other stuff investors normally like people to provide when they're looking for money," he said. "Then I grill them about the content, just to reassure myself they've done their homework."

He puffed at his stogie, thought a moment, then, using the cigar as a pointer, he said, "But it's all wishful thinking, fantasy stuff, projection, which is meaningless in itself, until the business is actually running. Then you work like hell to achieve your targets, and make the plan a self-fulfilling prophecy." Leaning forward over his desk, he drew Kevin into his secret. "But if I'm still interested after looking at a guy's paperwork, and hearing his defence of it, I'll take him to lunch, and watch how he eats, how much he drinks, how he treats the restaurant staff, that sort of thing." He paused to confirm Kevin was with him. "If I'm still interested after lunch, I'll have my wife invite him and his wife to dinner, so she can look him over, and I'll put a detective on him—"

"A detective?!" Kevin blurted out. "Isn't that a bit extreme?"

"Not really," he shrugged, and sat back in his chair. "I want to know if he cheats on his wife. I figure a guy who will cheat one partner, will cheat any partner..."

Mac rose from his chair. "Kevin, wisdom like that isn't new or original, though it seems to be something that has to be learned over and over again," he said.

"How so?" Kevin asked.

"In 1220, Genghis Khan is reported to have said, 'A man who is once faithless can never be trusted.' He said it just after capturing the city of Samarkand following what is considered one of the greatest strategic manoeuvres in military history," Mac said. "Then the Khan ordered the slaughter of 50,000 mercenary defenders of the city who had deserted their employers and joined the Mongol hordes to save themselves."

Kevin thought on that for a moment. "I prefer the idea of putting a private detective on a person, Mac."

CHAPTER SIX

Proprietorship? Partnership? Corporation?

1995, The Conference: *Day One, Conference Luncheon*

"He was right out of a poster for a western movie, whipcord thin, loose-jointed, with a rolling bow-legged walk, and this droopy kind of moustache that framed a real charmer of a smile," Kevin said. "And there were two younger versions of him with him."

"In Vancouver?" asked Jimmy Baldwin, the economic development officer for the Cape Breton Development Association.

Lunch had been set up as an informal talk session, with working groups around each table. Kevin knew Kieron had an agenda when he found himself at a table with his brother, Monique Pelletier, Jimmy Baldwin, Brenda Bashford, and Jill Johnston, who was attending the conference to research an article she was doing on the incubator program for *Canadian Enterprise* magazine.

Kevin nodded. "They were on their way back to Alberta from a business trip to Tokyo."

"What kind of business would three cowboys have in Tokyo?" Monique Pelletier asked.

"Well, in their case, they were settling the details on a million-dollar-plus deal with a Japanese film producer to provide and care for stock to be used in the biggest horse movie to be made in North America since the '60s," Kevin said. "The movie was called *Heaven and Earth*—"

"Yes, about the feuding warlords," Monique said.

"I think all Japanese period movies are about feuding warlords," Kevin said drily. "But you're right, that's the one. A $50-million epic, with all the battle scenes shot in Alberta, about five, six years ago, I think." He thought for a moment. "Yeah, just before I sold A Chip." He nodded. "Anyway, this guy Dusty Hughes was in charge of buying, training and taking care of 800 horses for five months."

"And he wanted a computer so he could manage the horses?" Monique asked.

Kevin shook his head. "The two younger cowboys were his sons D.J., who was his assistant, and Dwayne, the horse stunt co-ordinator," Kevin said. "D.J. had a commerce degree from the University of Lethbridge, and, on the trip back from Tokyo, he finally convinced his father to computerize the business operations of the family corporation, which owned the ranch, the film outfitting company, and two other ancillary entertainment and recreation-related businesses."

"A commerce degree? A cowboy?" Monique wondered.

"Can't judge a book, etcetera, Monique," Kevin said. "I was doing one of my store visits, and they so intrigued me, I served them myself."

"It doesn't make sense," Jimmy Baldwin said. "Why would they buy the computer in Vancouver and drag the stuff all the way to somewhere in Alberta?"

"Sometimes, you can get deals in Vancouver that you can't cut in Calgary," Kevin said.

"But still, carrying a complete computer system all the way to—" Jimmy looked confused. "Where?"

"Longview," Kevin offered. "One of the prettiest pieces of real estate in southern Alberta…in a big valley that goes into the foothills and rolls right up to the Rockies."

"I gather you've been there, Kevin?" Kieron said.

"Been there? Kieron, I had the great pleasure of being escorted by Dusty Hughes, on horseback, to a gorgeous mountain lake in mid-summer, where we spent the better part of a hot, sunny day fishing, shooting bull, and generally goofing off in paradise…"

The Hughes had come to A Chip because of its reputation for having sales staff who spoke with, not at, the clientele. Kevin suggested that if they wanted to buy a system from his company, he would be glad to customize one for them in Calgary when he got there the next week, and he would give them as good, or better a deal than they could get anywhere else. Kevin also asked some critical questions about computer use in the ranching and farm business. After the Hughes left the store, he got on the company's electronic mail system and sent a message to all store managers across the country asking them to research the potential market demand in their area for agriculture-related computer management systems.

"And that is why A Chip Off The Old Block was such a success," Kieron beamed proudly at his brother. "Kevin had a tight vision of his core market, and serviced it well, but never passed up opportunities he saw along the way."

"Well, the agricultural market for computers didn't have any strength until about '89, because of client resistance. Since then, it has exploded," Kevin said. "But we had already started setting up our rural marketing network. Merchants in small towns surrounding the urban centres where we were located became our first-contacts people, equipped with brochures and introductory product information packages we prepared. They got referral fees on any sales we made."

"Why not just advertise?" Monique asked.

"Well, Dusty's wife, Joanne, gave me an education in rural buying habits," Kevin said. "And many of them are influenced by their discomfort with the cities being too large, noisy and crowded. So, they'll buy locally first, if something is available. If not, they buy in the nearest town, if what they want is available. Going to the city to shop is a last resort."

"So you went to them," Kieron said.

"Not quite," Kevin said. "I wanted to get our company name as a source of equipment, software and support into the potential purchaser's mind before he or she even began the shopping process."

"Oh, so you met them halfway," Monique said. "Now how do we develop in other Canadians the spirit of entrepreneurship you showed?"

"I'm fascinated by how differently we see things," Kevin said. "You, from government, see this as just another problem in social engineering. You know: see a problem; come up with a solution; sell the minister on the concept; prepare a budget; get the program approved. I see it differently, as the challenge of getting from product concept to closing the sale." He shrugged. "Maybe it is, maybe it isn't a social engineering problem. I believe it isn't. We can't invent people with enterprise, touch them with a magic wand, and POOF!, they're entrepreneurs. *We can only provide the information people need to liberate their imaginations and find the spirit within themselves. Then they have to do it themselves."*

"I detect a certain distrust of government participation in the economy," Monique said warily.

"No, government is a necessary partner to business and the people," Kevin admitted. "The partner that must ensure internal peace and order, and defend us from outside intervention. Government also has a part to play as the lubricant between the elements of society that all want a piece of the good life, and think that there is a limited number of pieces to go around."

"So you would like business to operate without any controls?" Monique asked. "Again the American model."

"No, I'm advocating that you leave us alone to become the best we can be, the same way we must let people make themselves the best they can be," Kevin said. "But government must not be the one that decides what or who is best, or takes care of people, because this erodes initiative, and relieves us—individuals and businesses—of individual responsibility. This is the messy situation we have now, and it isn't working. If you think it's working, ask someone who isn't."

"Sounds like a co-operative capitalism," Jill Johnston ventured.

"Call it what you like, Jill," Kevin said. "But we must stop operating under the fallacy in this country that those in positions of authority, power and responsibility—whether they're business leaders, government people or some kind of expert—are privy to some special wisdom."

"Can I quote you on that?" Jill said, pulling a notebook from her bag.

Monique spluttered: "But we have the resources—"

"Yes, to you, Jill. And Monique, no question you have the resources to write the rules of the game," Kevin interrupted. "So you control the game, but your business is administration, which is not the business game. Business has one function only, to make a profit from buying and selling things. All other administrative functions must be subordinated to that task. To ignore that reality is to work against us. Quote me on that, too, Jill."

"Right," she said as she scribbled madly in her notebook. "Business has one function only, to make a profit from buying and selling things."

"Good," he said and turned back to Monique, his features creased with exasperation. How could he explain business to Monique without insulting her? He saw what she didn't see, that as a bureaucrat who wasn't motivated by profit, she had only an intellectual or academic view of business. So how could she possibly teach, or preach, business principles, practices, or perspectives to others? How could he get her to understand?

"So, you are saying only business leaders have the authority and experience to have all the answers for business," Monique insisted.

"Not at all, Monique," Kevin laughed. "If anything, we usually come up with answers that serve our own purposes, but not necessarily any greater good—just like any citizen. But there's this notion in this country that wealth implies wisdom, so we have louder voices that are sometimes heard more clearly in the councils of power. Some of us shut up, and learn…and there are some things we can learn from you, as much as from anyone else. The key, for me at least, is to select ideas and lessons as if I was cherry picking— take only the ripe ones."

Monique had no reply. Kevin searched for a way to finally drive home his point, that theory is important, but it serves best when tempered by practical experience. He remembered a story that came out of China's Cultural Revolution of the late '60s, launched when Mao Tse-tung worried that an emerging elite class of intellectuals was challenging his revolution, his regime, and his rule. A group of students dragged a professor of metallurgy from his lecture hall at Peking University to a machine shop, and demanded that he pull out a piece of molybdenum-chrome tubing from among a bunch of scrap stock on a work bench. He couldn't.

"He was a leader in his field. An expert. He could describe the processing of the metal, its specific gravity, the tensile strength of the metal…all of its characteristics," Kevin said. "He knew it all, had all the answers, but couldn't point to a piece of moly-chrome tubing when faced with it."

. . . .

1990: *A Lecture Hall, Oswego College*

"...so, for the next few weeks, we'll be working on an area of management I call trade skills," Kevin said. "And they're all dedicated to the most important goal of business, which is to sell things at a profit, and to ensure there is a profit by earning more than you spend."

"Well, that's obvious," John Tan called out.

"Is it, John?" Kevin asked. "Tell me, what is a bank's business?"

"Mac could probably answer that better than I can," John suggested.

"You think so?" Kevin asked as he turned and nodded at Mac.

"Why, managing money," Mac said.

"Close, but no cigar, Mac. Managing money is a function," Kevin said. "The bank is actually selling data processing services. Money happens to be the commodity about which it processes the data. When a bank takes in a cheque as a deposit, it processes information. We haven't yet got to the point where banks are charging deposit fees, except for commercial accounts, but if you write a cheque, there's a service charge. The charge is for data processing."

"Well, you definitely aren't paying for the 'service' in that service charge," Anne Porter offered. "I always feel like I'm being herded, you know, through the bank's velvet rope trail."

"We aren't here today to criticize the banks," Kevin said. "What we're concerned with now is an introduction to specific methods of doing business."

"I thought we did that with the surveys and the reports," John said.

"No, those were the *types* of business operations," Kevin said as he went to an overhead projector. "I'm talking about the legal constructions of businesses."

He switched the machine on and the screen read:

METHODS OF CARRYING ON BUSINESS

There are three ways to carry on business:

    Proprietorships

    Partnerships

    Corporations

All other ways of carrying on business, such as joint ventures, limited partnerships and the like, are variations on these methods.

"There you are, folks, the essence of capitalism, the three methods of carrying on business," Kevin said, gesturing at the screen as he paced across the front of the room. "Each of these methods has implications to you when it comes to your approach to money and tax management."

. . . .

FROM THE TRANSCRIPT OF **ADMINISTRATIVE HEADACHES,** A WORKSHOP AT THE 1995 OSWEGO COLLEGE SELF-EMPLOYMENT CONFERENCE *(Available from Allied Tape and Transcription Services Ltd., c/o Oswego College, $5.00 a copy, sales taxes included.)*

SUSAN MANYFINGERS: "Why couldn't we just go into business?" I kept asking my classmates back in '90. Everyone was encouraging, positive, motivational—everything you could want in a learning environment. I think one of Kevin's favorite lines should become the program's motto: *You can do anything. You just have to decide what you want to do, equip yourself to do it, then do it.*

Equipping myself wasn't as bad as I made it out to be as I bitched and moaned my way through the first weeks of the program. Mac always said not to worry. We're all soldiers at heart, unhappy unless we have something to complain about.

Well, I hated the administration of finances and tax stuff. Actually, I hated all the administrative stuff! I have, however, learned to deal with it, one day at a time, with all the patience I can dredge up. That's what I learned from the Oswego program: Use my brains. Use my patience.

But that doesn't mean I have to like the administrative stuff that's involved with business! (That's why I pay professionals to do most of it for me.) I remember the day I shouted that at Kevin in class, and he agreed with me.

"You hate it so much because you see it as a chore," he said. "And you haven't even been doing it day to day yet. You need to find the angle that makes doing business so much fun and so enjoyable, that the boring parts become tolerable. Like targeting, cutting and closing deals."

"Huh?" I said, caught in mid-tantrum, and wishing I had been more elegant in my outburst.

"Do you think *I* like *all* this business stuff?" Kevin asked. "Sitting behind a desk pushing paper around, smiling at bankers who are trained to either kowtow or browbeat you, depending on what you're worth to them? Do I like that? It's someone's fantasy that the wealthy and successful enjoy every little bit of administrative trivia..."

"It's my fantasy, Kevin," John volunteered. "You're super rich, so you make the bankers squirm."

"Not worth the effort," Kevin said. "They're only functionaries of a system that's just as bureaucratic as government, and just as distant from the real essence of business—trade—as big business is."

Damn, that man's good! I wish he'd run a sales course. Anyway, he went on and told us a story about this guy he knew in London, Ontario, Stan Blanchard. They went to business school together, then Stan stayed in London and became a bailiff, of all things. Besides his regular work of locking up businesses or tenants in rent arrears, or repossessing cars from people who didn't pay their loans or leases, and a whole bunch of other things involved with getting people who skip out on their obligations to meet them, this guy had contracts to collect late and delinquent taxes, and a few other municipal billings, in London, St. Thomas and a half dozen municipalities in the area. He made one bank manager an extremely happy man by putting many millions of dollars through that branch each year, and turning it into one of the most profitable in southwestern Ontario. Stan's success, however, had the unfortunate effect of slowing down the manager's career.

Stan had spent a lot of time working with that bank manager, negotiating a reduced service charge package because of the amount of money and transactions he ran through the bank. Now people don't usually understand you can do that, because the banks usually send most of us notices of new fees when they add to or increase service charges, and act as if these are the prices charged to everyone. They act like little tinpot dictators to most of their depositors, but if you're pushing $20 million through a commercial account each year, you represent many dollars in fees to the bank. You're in a position to negotiate those fees, and show your appreciation by staying, or to express dissatisfaction by putting feet to your money and finding another, more agreeable, bank.

Well, Stan liked the deals he had made with that bank, and liked having that particular manager to work with, and even felt he had been a part of the manager's training in what business is really about. He mentioned it when the bank's regional vice-president, also a Western business school graduate, took him to lunch one day to say how pleased the bank was to have his business.

Stan told the VP how unhappy he would be if the manager was transferred any time in the next three years. It would be too soon, as he had just finished teaching him how to do business and would hate to waste time having to train another person. Why, he might even move his accounts somewhere else, to show how unhappy he was that the bank didn't understand the need for strong personal and business relations with clients. After all, the bankers all had jobs; they didn't understand the value of an independent businessman's time. They got paid whether or not business was transacted, while the independent was left counting time wasted and money lost.

The regional VP got the message. The manager, an ambitious fellow eager to climb the corporate ladder as far as he could go, remained branch manager for five more years, much longer than the usual rotation.

"There are three lessons here," Kevin said in concluding the story. "One, the banks profit from your trade. Make them work for it, or at least try to make them work for it. Second, banks don't know what your business is about. You're the expert. You have to educate them. That way, when someone tells you something is policy, and you ask to see the policy, and you still don't like the policy, you can find someone who will bend the rules to meet your needs."

"That's only two," Brenda objected when Kevin stopped talking and began pacing.

"Well, I'm looking for diplomatic wording," Kevin smiled.

"Why start now?" Stan Everett said to the delighted laughter of his classmates. "You've been on a shoot-from-the-hip roll for weeks."

Kevin smiled ruefully, and nodded. "Okay, then... The third is, don't let a banker become your boss," he said. "If you can do it, raise money anywhere but from a bank. If you have to, use bank money to provide your short-term revolving credit for operations, but stay away from long-term debt from banks—from any institutions—for start-up, *for your capitalization*. For one thing, interest on debt is a business killer. For another, the moment you're into financial institutions for money, especially banks, they believe they own you."

"But what about the saying 'Owe $1,000 and it's your problem, owe a million dollars and it's the bank's problem.'?" Brenda asked.

"An interesting cliche, but a banker told me as far back as '83, 'A million ain't what it used to be.'" Kevin said. "They'll shut down anybody who owes them money and looks like they might default—and I've seen them shut down businesses that *were* succeeding, but not fast enough, or not generating enough in fees for the bank to bother hanging in. Like I said, owe banks money, and they think they own you."

"Sure, because they get you to pledge everything you own as security," John said.

"That's not the issue, John," Kevin said. "Once you're in debt to a bank, you're dancing to its tune. Your ability to act quickly on opportunity becomes restricted."

"He's right," Mac said. "But you have to understand it isn't personal. It's the banker's policy: Cut risk."

"Which might ensure banks make money, but doesn't contribute to business development and overall economic health," Kevin said. "I know we can't all avoid this particular avenue of raising money, but try. You could apply for a loan with guarantees from the federal government under the Small Business Loans Act, but I've heard bankers say they hate government guarantees, because then people don't work hard enough to meet their obligations, because they know the feds will cover for them."

"Maybe the banks would finance a national chain of for-profit debtors prisons," John quipped.

"Try them," Kevin said. "If you provide them with a credible business plan—" He shrugged. "You never know. Anyway, you won't see banks eager to lend under the Small Business Loans Act until they're stuffed full of savings, interest rates are low, we're in the middle of a recession, and borrowing levels drop dramatically."

The class degenerated into a bitch-about-banks session before Kevin could get it under control, so he called a coffee break, to give us time to vent and settle down. When we got back, he was all formal and organized, and he addressed the methods of carrying on business. I had to leave for a dentist's appointment I had waited weeks to get, so I got John Tan's notes on the session.

I could tell he was trained as an engineer. He took neat, complete notes and even wrote himself notes in brackets on things to follow up.

. . . .

1990: *John Tan's Class Notes*

PROPRIETORSHIPS

A proprietorship is a business conducted by an individual alone, and without using a limited company, for the purpose of making a profit. The profit angle is important should Revenue Canada ever challenge whether your business is actually a business, just a hobby, or a loss-creating vehicle to dodge taxes.

Proprietorships require no legal filings except the trade name under which you operate, which can be done with a provincial corporate registry. This protects the name under which you're doing business. Proprietorship is the simplest form of business, involves the least amount of government interference, and is usually the best method to choose for the early stages of a business.

(Check out with an accountant: If you have income from another source while you're developing your business, business losses can be deducted against your other income. Cited in class as the major advantage of the proprietorship: the profit or loss, especially the loss, is recorded on your own return as an offset against other income.)

The major disadvantage of operating a sole proprietorship is you face unlimited liability, because you own all the assets of the business and are personally responsible for all of its liabilities. Any legal action could be taken against the trade name or you, but in either case you, the sole proprietor, are the responsible entity.

Tax treatment in a proprietorship works this way:
1. You (the business) earn the gross income.

2. Expenses are deducted against gross income.
3. Net income is what you then report in the income section of your personal tax return, and whatever is left after personal deductions and tax credits is taxed at *the appropriate individual tax rate.*

PARTNERSHIPS

A partnership is a business relationship between two or more parties doing business without using a limited company. Most of what applies to sole proprietorships applies in partnerships.

(Especially the tax implications. If, as in the proprietorship, you have a regular income from another source while you're developing your business, your share of business losses can be deducted against your other income. So, investors who put money into an unincorporated partnership in development, when expenses are high, can claim those expenses as losses against their personal income.)

An important distinction is that all assets and liabilities are held 'jointly and severally' by all partners. This means all liabilities of a partnership are the liabilities of each partner, and each partner is the lawful agent of the other partners. So, any partner can enter into agreements, and incur liabilities for the company, and each partner is fully liable for all debts of the partnership. This can be limited by a partnership agreement, and any partner incurring a liability must then inform the party with whom the liability is being incurred about the agreement, which means the one incurring the liability would be assuming it individually.

Tax treatment in a partnership works this way:
1. You and your partner(s) (the partnership) earn the gross income.
2. Expenses are deducted against gross income.
3. Whatever is your percentage share in the net earnings from the partnership comes to you as all or part of your net income from the partnership.
4. Net income is what you then report in the income section of your personal tax return, and whatever is left after personal deductions and tax credits is taxed *at the appropriate individual tax rate.*

(So we're talking similar tax treatment to proprietorships here. Kevin says we're going to talk about operating business in partnership with other people a little later on. Danielle, his wife, is coming to help teach that session. He also suggested looking into income splitting when you're in business. This is a technique whereby an individual who makes enough to be in a high tax bracket, and has a spouse, or equivalent to a spouse in a lower tax bracket, can split the income with the spouse to get the most advantageous treatment.)

NOTE TO SUSAN: Here's a quick example to illustrate, then you can ask about it again on your own. If you have an income taxable at a high rate, and your spouse has a lower income taxed at a low rate, you can reduce your total tax exposure by splitting the income with your spouse. The bite on two incomes of $30,000 is significantly less than that on $20,000 and $40,000 combined. How?

All taxes combined on income up to $30,000 average about 25 per cent across country. All taxes combined on income from $30,000 to $60,000 range from 40 to 45 per cent, depending on the province. Tax rates on all dollars from $60,000 up range from 45 to 50 per cent depending on the province.

- So, you make $20,000. Your tax bite at 25 per cent is $5,000.
- Your spouse makes $40,000, and pays 25 per cent, or $7,500, on the first $30,000, and, in your province, 42.5 per cent, or $4,250, on the next $10,000, for a total of $11,750
  Together, you pay $16,750 in taxes.
- If you split the income, and each pay 25 per cent on $30,000, you pay $15,000 in total, a saving of $1,750. The savings become greater with larger incomes to split.

Income splitting also increases your spouse's income levels, which means he or she has a higher RRSP contribution threshold, so you and your spouse can deposit more in tax-sheltered savings plans.

CORPORATIONS

Though normally called a *corporation,* the formal name of the third method of doing business is 'limited liability corporation', an entity created under law, which, essentially, has the status of a legal entity on par with a 'human being'. The word 'limited' establishes that under law the liability of the corporation's shareholders is limited to the amount each initially paid for the shares, which means if the business dies, the loss is limited to the share purchase price.

Both federal and provincial governments have jurisdiction over corporations, and we have the option of incorporating federally or provincially. If you incorporate provincially in your home province, but want to do business in another province, you must register to do business in that second province, but don't have to create a new entity. If you incorporate federally, you still have to register in your home province and any other province to conduct business through a permanent establishment in those jurisdictions; in some cases, you might even find it makes more sense, though it's costly, to incorporate in each jurisdiction. The only advantage to incorporating federally seems to be that the name of a federally incorporated company gets priority protection.

The incorporation process works this way: Pick a name. Have a name search done. If the search comes up with no conflicts, you do the paperwork, file it, and pay your fees with the appropriate federal or provincial agency. The registrar of businesses still has the option of accepting or rejecting a name because it might encroach upon another name. If you have a name similar to a provincially incorporated name in another jurisdiction, chances are the registrar will still accept your name. If, however, your chosen name is close to that of a federally incorporated company's name, the registrar will likely reject it.

(The assumption underlying this name business, Kevin said, is that the operators of a federally incorporated company anticipate going national.)

As a corporation is created under authority of law, there is a prescribed method of incorporation, which requires the creators to comply with certain requirements and filings of forms (yes, in multiple copies). Once created, the corporation's status must be maintained through additional filings. The specific filings vary from jurisdiction to jurisdiction, so you have to take this into account when planning your incorporation strategies. This method of doing business requires the most contact with regulatory agencies.

Tax treatment in a corporation works this way:
1. The corporation earns the gross income.
2. Expenses are deducted against gross income.
3. The business profit is taxed at the corporate rate.
4. Profits distributed to you as dividends are personal income, taxed at a special dividend rate.

5. Income from the business, if you are an employee paid a salary, is subject to withholding tax and other payroll deductions. The corporation, however, deducts what it pays you as a business expense, so it isn't taxed twice.

6. If you work as an employee of the company, you manage your personal income just as you would if you worked full time for someone else.

(The key issue here is that if you're operating a one- or two-person corporation, you should avoid mixing business and personal funds. That means separate bank accounts, and a clear paper trail on what is corporate money and what is personal, otherwise, preparing a profit and loss statement, part of the year-end reporting package, becomes a nightmare.)

CHAPTER SEVEN

Deep in the Heart of Taxes

1995, The Conference: *Day One, A Break Between Sessions*

"Kevin…" Monique Pelletier said again.

"Hmm," Kevin looked up at Monique and Jimmy Baldwin. "Oh, Monique. Jimmy. I'm sorry, I was thinking about something."

"Something so important that you were in another world?" Monique asked as she gestured at the empty chairs around the table.

"Of course, please," Kevin nodded. "It is important," he said as they set down their brown attache cases, what he called the bureaucrat's badge. "My wife and I are cooking up something, and it's just about ready to be unveiled."

"Ah, gourmet capitalism, with a soupçon of mystery," Monique smiled as she seated herself.

Kevin chuckled.

"We must speak, Kevin," Monique said. "The little tensions that exist between us, are they personal, or are you like this with all government employees?"

Kevin reddened with embarrassment. "I must apologize. I know you're well meaning. You have your job to do, as I have mine. Though I get my back up at your persistence in dismissing the realities of business."

"We just look at the world through different screens," Jimmy Baldwin said.

"True, and I believe you folks are working against us," Kevin said.

"Now why do you think that?" Monique asked.

"Because you're trying to recreate in miniature a world that doesn't exist any more, and wasn't particularly healthy or efficient when it did," Kevin said. "The Big Business model, where mega-corporations created large job rolls, was a burst of post-war recovery growth you…ah, politicians and bureaucrats…promoted and encouraged. When it petered out, government jumped on the small-

125

business bandwagon and the idea that a lot of businesses that employ up to 100 people would save the country."

"But these are the trends we see, what we discern as the future," Monique insisted.

"Flavor of the month thinking, Monique. They're only part of the picture," Kevin said. "There are other options that aren't being explored for their possibilities, perhaps are being discouraged, because you're focusing your attention elsewhere."

"These options are...what?" Jimmy wondered.

"Well, at a conference last year, I met a fellow named Dr. Ray Rasker, an economist who conducted a study published as The Wealth of Nature by the Wilderness Society. He offers another view of life in the post-industrial world that has substance, but it's being ignored as a model..."

Rasker studied the economy of the Greater Yellowstone Region, almost 34 million acres in 20 counties where the states of Montana, Wyoming and Idaho intersect. One of his concerns was the impact of partial or complete mine closures, restriction of lumbering, and cutbacks, or complete closure of mineral and timber processing facilities in the area. The common belief was the area would become a post-industrial wasteland, essentially depopulated as residents fled the lack of jobs. The few remaining residents of the region would be consigned to lives of unproductive, meaningless poverty.

Rasker found the opposite happened. The Region's economy did not collapse, and not only did economic activity remain stable, but it grew, dramatically, for a number of reasons. The Region, which boasts startling scenery, and a dramatic grouping of national and state parks, was a tourist destination, made more attractive because the mines, smelters and mills weren't messing up the landscape, and loggers weren't clear-cutting the land. So tourism increased.

Besides being a tourist destination, the area became an internal immigration destination—Americans fleeing urban sprawl and all of its ills in the mid-'80s, began moving to rural locations, and the towns of the Yellowstone Region became primary destinations. This migration was aided by communications technology that ensured these people could stay in touch with as much, or as little of the urban experience as they cared for. This same technology allowed them to do business by fax, modem and computer over phone lines and satellite links, and some mass market American publications about home businesses and entrepreneurship have, since 1988, been chronicling the phenomenon of urban escapers working in places like Bozeman, Montana, while serving the needs of clients in Chicago, New York, and Los Angeles.

These escapers brought new skills and capital, and created, or caused to be created, subordinate service work. One example he cites is of an independent financial planner who moved into the area from a large city, and serves clientele in the Region. He provides a full range of financial services locals formerly had to drive to the nearest big city to take care of, taking at least two full days or more away from their work. He works with the locals, advises them on investments and a range of retirement planning options, and places their investments for them. He hired a local woman to run his office for him, because he's out in the area a great deal. So, the net gain to the Region was one new family, which, by settling from outside the area, brought new money into the Region, generated economic spin-offs from that family, the new business, one new job, and the spin-offs from that business and job.

After his meeting with Rasker, Kevin had added a page to his office daybook, a three-ring binder in which he kept a copy of his personal development plan, his business plan, and a jumble of notes he accumulated each day about things to look into, ideas to pursue, and stray thoughts. He would read the critical documents each day before following his day's schedule of work, and the new page was a new grouping of ideas—some new, some old—triggered by Rasker that Kevin felt were important to spend a little time thinking about every day if he were to become a better businessman, teacher, and investor. It read:

1. Expertise is transportable, has value, and adds value to economic activity.
2. Consumer need exists wherever population exists.
3. 500 jobs are 500 jobs, whether provided by one company, three companies or 250 companies.
4. Value-added economic growth is value added whether it comes from processing raw materials, processing ideas, or providing for the needs of a local population.

5. Electronic and communications technology can be used to create virtual cities in large thinly populated areas, creating the critical mass necessary for them to become viable economic zones able to create value-added growth.
6. Opportunity exists anywhere, and business can be done effectively, anywhere, given existing economic and communications infrastructures.
7. The traditional concept of factory has to give way to a new vision. The mind, the computer, the one-person workshop, or the workshop where a few people work, is, essentially, a factory, a place in which things are created for sale.

"...but, surely, you need industry to create wealth," Monique insisted.

"No question we do," Kevin said. "But break the chains of convention. Think of the economy as what it has been—a mix of big businesses, a lot of small businesses, and many micro-businesses."

Kevin paused to check that Monique and Jimmy were following him. They nodded.

"Now, look at what the economy is becoming," he urged. "A mix of some slimmed-down big businesses, a lot of small businesses, and a huge number of micro-businesses, some of which exist solely to be low-cost service providers to the other businesses. Think of them all networking, the micros, possibly spread around the country, coming together in project teams, partnerships or joint ventures of professionals in business, connected by phone, fax and satellite, contracted and financed by the bigger companies to carry out specific projects."

"The virtual corporation," Jimmy Baldwin said, almost breathlessly. "Now I understand the concept."

"Ouch, I hate jargon," Kevin said. "It's too often used as an excuse for real understanding of a situation. However, if you want to put it in those terms, yes, and we must include technical skills in the area of knowledge work."

"And you want us to move in this direction?" Monique asked.

"Move? No! March resolutely, as part of the strategy to promote industrial renewal, yes!" Kevin said. "Look, we know what you're here for. You and your steering committee have to give your respective ministers a portrait of what you think the future will be, and advise them on how to restructure government services and roles. I don't envy you. You have to play oracle on government policies for the next 10 or 15 years, when we're sometimes stuck for ideas on coping with the next 10 or 15 minutes."

"Exactly, Kevin, which is why I must enlist your help," Monique said. "Besides listening to the speakers, I have been speaking with your graduates. You have an incredible number who are running their own businesses successfully."

"Yeah, but we've also lost a lot who decided the risks or demands of running their own businesses weren't what they wanted."

"It is understandable," Monique said. "Change is difficult."

"Especially when you have to change yourself, drastically sometimes, to take a new direction in life," Kevin said. "And those grads who are in business got there because they had worked with a mix of academic and professional businesspeople as instructors, who helped them develop certain skills and attitudes, and encouraged them to try, without encouraging any specific project or business direction."

"But such ambiguity…" Monique marvelled. "What is the spark?"

"Well, that cowboy in Alberta I told you about was a championship rodeo competitor. He lives a dream life in the foothills, cattle ranching, and running an outfitting business supplying horses and equipment for TV programs and movies," Kevin said. "He has even taken to going to the Caribbean for a holiday once a year." Kevin chuckled at the thought of Dusty on a beach somewhere, in a swimsuit, having a cold beer and wearing his cowboy hat and boots. "Dusty calls it 'the want', a bone-deep desire to live a particular way, and do the work to earn the money to pay the price of what you want."

"Do what you have to, so you can do what you want to," Jimmy shrugged. "How do you quantify that? How do you describe it?"

"If you're going to 'social engineer' for it, Jimmy, use the Oswego model," Kevin said. "My brother had the foresight to set it up as it is, with a concentration on teaching the practical. It doesn't mean our way is the only way, but we get results."

"Which is why I need you to come to Ottawa, and speak to my deputy minister, and then my minister," Monique said.

"And if you would, come to Cape Breton and speak to my association, and the people of the island," Jimmy said.

"Let's get through this weekend first," Kevin suggested.

....

1990: *A Lecture Hall, Oswego College*

"...and, as I said yesterday, there are other methods of carrying on business, but they're all variations on the proprietorship, partnership and corporation," Kevin said. "And before our guest tells you a few more things about the tax implications of business, I want to give you an important idea to consider." He looked around the room and smiled at everyone. *"Money spent to make a profit is a business expense.* That will take some thinking for you to understand and adjust to, but our guest will give you some insights into that. Brenda."

Brenda Bashford left her desk and came to the head of the lecture hall, as Kevin took her place.

"As you know, I've worked as a Certified General Accountant," she said. "That's why I would suggest you spend a few hours each year with a practising small business accountant and lawyer. The good ones will be current on the law as it affects their areas—they have to, to stay in business. This way, you can stay clear on the legal, financial, tax and estate planning implications of setting up and running your business."

"Do you have an interest in an accounting firm?" John Tan teased her.

"No, John," she said with a mock serious look. "I'm giving up the joys of accounting to feed the world." She couldn't sustain her stern look, and broke into laughter. When she got the laughter under control, she continued. "Kevin and I discussed how best to present this section of the discussion on taxes, so I asked the man who was my accounting instructor in my commerce program if he could come speak to us today. He's uniquely qualified to do this, because he works in his own consulting practice, advising small business operators on their business and personal financial planning. He has also written the standard text on small-business accounting and financial management, and his first mass-market paperback book on personal financial planning for small-business operators is being published next fall under the title, *Me, Millionaire*. I'm pleased to introduce Benjamin Chambers."

A tall, thin man with greying hair came to the lectern, and spread out some papers. He adjusted his wire rim glasses, knuckled the ends of his moustache, and eyed his audience for a moment before stepping away from the lectern.

"When I was invited here to speak to you, I thought long and hard about what you need to know about tax and related business matters, given that you are all planning to go into business," Chambers said in slow, measured tones. "I'm not here to make you accountants. Rather, as I understand, this program is designed to give you a knowledge foundation, and a place within which you can motivate yourselves and each other, with the encouragement of your instructors and guest speakers such as myself."

Members of the class nodded agreement.

"I think this is a marvellous concept, so, as I said, I thought hard, and prepared a short presentation for you of the basic information you need to know. Before I give it—" he nodded to Brenda who had seated herself in a front-row desk. "—I want to second Brenda's suggestion that whatever you know or don't know about financial management and tax issues, *consult with an accountant at least once a year*, to ensure you are up to date on information and moving ahead as you plan. Remember, the rules can change with the turn of a government budget change."

. . . .

From Mac's class notes on Benjamin Chambers's talk

Chambers reinforces the point that a major advantage of the *proprietorship* is that a profit, or loss, especially a loss, say during a start-up period, is recorded on your own return as an offset against other income.

The downside to being in a proprietorship is that you have *unlimited* liability, which means everything you own is at risk if you get sued for some reason. This is why some people think they need to incorporate. In general, however, even if you incorporate, if you borrow money from a lending institution, you'll likely have to provide personal guarantees, including pledging real property such as a home, and this will negate much of the advantage of limited liability.

On the other hand, limited liability protection can be important if you're involved in any industry where there are potential losses from customers, bystanders, whoever. For example, if you own a restaurant and someone dies from ptomaine poisoning, you might not be completely covered by your insurance, especially if a lot of people die in one day from eating spoiled food. So limited liability can be important as it can protect your personal savings and property.

A *partnership* is very much like a proprietorship, except you have several people involved, and the income, or loss, is split in a profit-sharing ratio. It's probably useful to point out that here in Canada, we have a tax system that does not couple the incomes of a husband and wife. As such, the key point is to always try to use the low tax bracket twice.

Chambers reinforced and restated some of what we were told by Kevin last week. The key is to understand that the first $30,000 of income is taxed at a combined (federal and provincial) rate of about 25 per cent (it varies from province to province). From $30–$60,000, the combined rate is from 40 to 45 per cent including all surtaxes, flat rate taxes, etc., and above $60,000, you can count on giving the government from 45 to a bit more than 50 per cent on these incremental dollars, depending on the province.

The ability to *split income* between spouses is key, because the taxes on two incomes of $30,000 are significantly less than the tax on one income of $60,000. We discussed the example we used in the previous session, as illustration.

The test of a valid partnership between a husband and wife would be the capital invested, and time and effort expended. So, if I put in $50,000 and my wife puts in $10,000, it would be hard on that basis alone to justify a 50-50 split of profits. This is where time and effort considerations come in. If I can show that even though the capital is unequal, my wife puts in the same time and effort, or more, then, in that situation, maybe a 60-40 split of profits would be acceptable. So we have some latitude for planning based on the tests of time and effort and capital contributions.

In the case of a *corporation,* a key point to emphasize is that

I can set up the share structure so my wife can hold shares in the company without being active. In this case, she couldn't be remunerated by way of a salary, but the corporation could pay dividends to her on her stock, and it could pay significant dividends on a nominal investment. What I would do is have separate classes of shares, and so I, for example, as the active person in the corporation, and paid a salary by the corporation, would subscribe to Class A shares, and she would subscribe to class B shares, and dividends would be paid on the B shares only. This is a tax gimmick, but it appears to work.

The rule of thumb is that you don't bother incorporating, leaving limited liability issues aside, unless you're making profits greater than what you need to live on. This is because, if you don't leave money in the corporation, there isn't a whole lot of point to incorporation.

The point Chambers stresses is what he calls one of the most underrated advantages of incorporation—*the ability to pay off financing liabilities with cheaper after-tax dollars*. It works this way. A private corporation that earns income from an active business operation pays, on average, across Canada, a combined (federal and provincial) tax rate of approximately 20 per cent on annual business income up to $200,000 a year.

So, let's assume my company earns $50,000 after paying all business expenses, but before I draw anything in salary. Let's assume I draw $30,000 to cover my living expenses, which are about $20,000 and a bit after tax. So there's another $20,000—the profit—left over. If I'm unincorporated, that extra $20,000 would be taxed at about 40 per cent, so I'd only have 60 per cent of the extra $20,000, or *$12,000*, available to pay off my capital borrowings, whether it was to the bank, or somebody in my family who lent me money.

On the other hand, if I incorporate, and the company makes a profit of $50,000, and I draw a salary of $30,000, the remaining $20,000 is only taxed at the small business rate of 20 per cent. So, the company is left with 80-cent dollars, $16,000, compared with $12,000, to pay off debt. Now most people don't realize this is an advantage, but the ability to pay off debt with cheap dollars is really important.

KEY POINT: Pay off principal with after-tax dollars!

Another key point to consider here is how to pay for *disallowed expenses*—those expenses incurred to do business that can't be deducted from income. For example, club memberships in any club that provides dining, recreational and sporting facilities is not a permissible expense, or that portion of entertainment expenses the government says we can't claim against income.

If you're going to have a disallowed expense, you'd rather have it disallowed when the tax rate on the money you spend is 20 per cent than when it is 40 or 50 per cent. For example, assume I wanted to join a club, and the membership fee is $800. If I'm in a 50 per cent bracket, I need $1,600 in pre-tax income to net $800 to pay the club membership. My company on the other hand, could earn $1,000, pay 20 per cent corporate tax, and use the $800 retained profits to pay the disallowed membership fee. So, that's another advantage of incorporating.

Incorporation isn't a difficult process; it only involves filling out and filing certain forms. Maybe you have to have a lawyer do it the first time, but after that, it's pretty easy to do yourself. With software and other technical aids, even doing corporate tax returns is not complicated. Corporations also give you a better sense of stability. Maybe that's a good marketing tool…you sort of feel like you've been around longer.

Chambers stressed the key to tax and financial management is that we have to think differently about managing the money we earn when we're in business for ourselves. For one thing, some of what were once personal expenses will now be legitimate business expenses, which brings to mind Kevin's, *"Money spent to make a profit is a business expense."*

What that means, though, is best learned by spending those few hours each year with an accountant, to stay up-to-date on the self-employed approach. For example, Chambers said, if I operate out of my home, part of my house operating costs such as property taxes, heating, other utilities, and specific expenses like putting in a portable fan or a space heater in the room where I work are tax deductible. If they aren't major costs, they become period costs— costs that can be written off as incurred.

Some *capital* costs are depreciable over time. Furniture, for example, depreciates at 20 per cent on a declining balance basis, except in the year of acquisition, when I'm allowed only half. On stuff like computers that depreciates more quickly, though, the rate is 30 per cent. What depreciation does is measure that these assets are in fact used up over time, but I also have to recognize I need to budget to eventually replace those particular assets.

Leasing is something to look into, even though the cost of leasing can be a little bit high, compared with using borrowed money, in terms of the implicit interest rate. Nevertheless it doesn't tie up credit in items purchased with borrowed money. In general, a lease allows a full write-off in the year the expenses are incurred.

One way or another, there will be deductions permitted for owning, or leasing, and operating an automobile in the course of carrying on a business. There are some restrictions on depreciating, or deducting costs for expensive vehicles.

Chambers recommended some books to consult, such as Henry B. Zimmer's *Canadian Tax and Investment Guide,* or the Price Waterhouse guide. He stressed, however, that we should each spend a few hours each year with an accountant who specializes in small business. He stressed the small business connection. An accountant with a large firm has an entirely different type of background. True, the large firms have small business branches, but we're paying more, for their offices, the lavishness, and so on, and he doesn't think we would get the same hands-on benefits as we would get from a small business accountant.

He went back to incorporation, and a final benefit of the small-business tax rate. It's really nice to make profits if you know the government isn't going to take away half. (Amen!)

If my company reaches the point where it no longer needs the 80-cent dollars for expansion, I can use the 80-cent dollars to create *investment capital* for myself within the corporation. I own the shares. I control the investment capital. That's the key point, and it's available to any savvy business operator. So, for example, my company can invest 80-cent dollars in stocks, bonds, real estate, gold, silver, antiques, even works of art, and the company owns this stuff, but it buys what I tell it to buy. Now the investment income is not taxed at the low 20 per cent rate, but the key point is that to have investment income, I have to first have investment capital, and investment capital is best created by the business owner through the use of 80-cent dollars.

The lesson here for us is: Work with the advice of professionals to ensure you're managing your tax and financial positions effectively. Chambers even said, "Never shirk paying your fair share of taxes—*and not one cent more.*" Then he read from the back cover of the General Income Tax Guide. There, in black and white, is the Declaration of Taxpayer Rights. At the bottom is a section which reads:

YOU HAVE THE RIGHT TO EVERY BENEFIT THE LAW ALLOWS.
You are entitled to arrange your affairs to pay the least amount of tax the law allows. We are committed to applying the tax laws in a consistent and fair manner. We will be firm with those who are guilty of tax evasion.

The key to effective management of all this stuff, Chambers said, is to have a good, complete, set of up-to-date records of income and expenses. He suggested it might even be the most important administrative task we have.

....

1990: *The Lecture Hall, Oswego College*

"Taxes at one rate if you're incorporated, and at another rate if you aren't," Anne Porter muttered as they broke for coffee. "The day I make $30,000 period, unincorporated or not, is the day I've made it."

"Be careful," Kevin warned. "If you ever think you've arrived, you're done for. Stay hungry and realize that achieving your goals is merely an excuse to re-evaluate them, put them in perspective, and establish a new set of goals."

"Is that how A Chip grew?" Brenda asked.

Kevin thought a moment, and nodded. "One set of goals at a time," he said, and smiled.

CHAPTER EIGHT

Your Friendly Paper Shedder

FROM THE TRANSCRIPT OF **SIMPLIFY THE PAPERWORK,** A PANEL DISCUSSION AND WORKSHOP AT THE 1995 OSWEGO COLLEGE SELF-EMPLOYMENT CONFERENCE *(Available from Allied Tape and Transcription Services Ltd., c/o Oswego College, $6 a copy, sales taxes included.)*

ANNE PORTER: I wonder why they let us loose from the public school system without teaching us the basics of building a household budget, or how to balance a checkbook. Teaching applied mathematics would probably make us all better thinkers. There's an order to numbers, and an order they impose on work when you have to work with them.

In the tax and money management seminars, Kevin stressed the need for us to develop the habit of keeping appropriate records— save all receipts, keep a mileage log in the car, and jot in your daytimer, or log, notes of important daily activities, where you've been, who you talked to. This is primarily to keep your finances and time under control, but, if you ever need them, you'll also have records—a paper trail—of your business affairs. And boy, did Kevin give us an earful about daytimers. He said under no circumstances should we work without one, and a hard copy one at that, like in a binder.

"I have yet to meet a computerized calendar program that I like," he said. "No one has yet mastered the art of making calling up a calendar page as easy or efficient as opening your daytimer. When that happens, I'll use it. Until then," he waved the tan harness leather binder he carries everywhere, one of those smaller six-ring jobs, "this is my bible. It shows me the path to righteous and businesslike behavior, and when and where I have to behave that way."

Kevin gave us a comprehensive Monthly Household Budget form to use for two purposes: one, to construct a budget to establish and analyze how much disposable income we use each month to maintain our lifestyles, and, two, how better to deploy that income. I use the form, and it works. I know what I need as a personal income, and can establish a realistic base income target for my business, and realistic ownership and financing structures.

The budget form is the first set of pages in the handouts.

MONTHLY HOUSEHOLD BUDGET

ANNUAL EXPENDITURES MADE:	AMOUNT	ANNUAL COST
MONTHLY		
Fitness club	_____	$ _____
SEMI-ANNUALLY		
Auto insurance	_____	_____
Life insurance	_____	_____
MEMBERSHIPS		
Union	_____	_____
Professional associations	_____	_____
Clubs	_____	_____
QUARTERLY		
Health care	_____	_____
ANNUALLY		
Home insurance	_____	_____
Vacations		
(set aside in savings)	_____	_____
Clothing	_____	_____
Auto registration	_____	_____
OTHER		
Religious holidays	_____	_____
Back to school	_____	_____
Tuition/books	_____	_____
Lessons/courses	_____	_____
Professional services	_____	_____
Other (specify)	_____	_____
TOTAL ANNUAL COSTS		_____
÷ 12 = MONTHLY COST		$ _____ 1

REGULAR
MONTHLY EXPENDITURES $/MONTH

HOUSING

    Rent/mortgage $ _____

    Condo fees   _____

    Taxes   _____

    Utilities (water, heat, phone, etc.)   _____

    Maintenance   _____

    Phone   _____

    Cable   _____

FOOD (groceries and non-food

    items purchased with groceries)   _____

    Restaurants/fast food   _____

CLOTHING

    Purchases   _____

    Laundry/drycleaning   _____

    Seasonal   _____

TRANSPORTATION

    Gas/oil/lubricants   _____

    Maintenance/repairs   _____

    Parking/public transit/cabs   _____

CREDIT PAYMENTS

    Auto lease/loan   _____

    Consumer loans   _____

    Charge accounts   _____

    Credit cards   _____

HEALTH COSTS

    Medical/dental   _____

    Optical   _____

    Prescription/non-prescription drugs   _____

SAVINGS/FINANCIAL SERVICES

    RRSP   _____

    Savings/investments   _____

    Bank service charges   _____

GROOMING/PERSONAL CARE

    Sundries   _____

    Barber/hairdresser   _____

    Allowances   _____

ENTERTAINMENT/INFORMATION
    Books/magazines   _____
    Newspapers   _____
    Entertainment/sports/hobbies   _____
    Babysitting   _____

OTHER
    Alimony   _____
    Child support   _____
    Daycare   _____
    Postage/stationery   _____
    Other (specify)   _____

TOTAL $ _____ 2

DISCRETIONARY
MONTHLY EXPENDITURES $/MONTH

SAVINGS $ _____

ENTERTAINMENT
    Sports equipment   _____

MISCELLANEOUS
    Charitable contributions   _____
    Pocket money/lunches/parking _____
    Children's programs/camps   _____

HOUSEHOLD
    Household goods, furniture, other _____
    Housing maintenance and repairs _____
    Housing decoration   _____
    Gardening supplies   _____
    Hired help   _____
    Subscriptions   _____

TOTAL $ _____ 3

TOTAL EXPENDITURES PER MONTH
    ADD LINES   1 _____
                             + 2 _____
                             + 3 _____

TOTAL MONTHLY EXPENDITURES $ _____ 4

After working with the budget form, and reviewing it annually, I understand what Kevin meant when he said, "If you don't know what you need to draw to live on, half your analysis is flawed."

Boy, thinking like a businessperson is different from being an employee. *You have to think about money, a lot, and how to make it, how to save it, how not to spend it if you don't have to, all the time, no matter how much you make.*

Now, the second purpose for this budget form is so I can break out from what I always held as lifestyle expenses those expenditures that can be legitimately claimed as business expenses. The way to do that is to construct a business expense template, which is the second set of pages in the handout.

SKILLS ON DEMAND TEMPORARIES LTD
09/31/95
EXPENSE CATEGORY LIST

Category	Description
A	ACCOUNTING, LEGAL, ETC.
A1	Accounting
A2	Legal
A3	Collection
A4	Consulting
B	ADVERTISING, PROMOTION
C	BAD DEBTS
D	BUSINESS TAX, FEES, ETC.
D1	Business taxes
D2	Fees
D3	Business licence
D4	Dues
E	CONVENTION EXPENSES
E1	Accommodations
E2	Convention registration
E3	Meals
E4	Per diem expense, non-meal
E5	Travel
E6	Tips/gratuities
F	DELIVERY, FREIGHT
G	EQUIPMENT RENTAL

H	INSURANCE
H1	Fire, theft, liability
H2	Disability
H3	Accident
I	INTEREST, BANK CHARGES
I1	Interest
I2	Bank charges
J	LIGHT, HEAT, WATER
J1	Light
J2	Heat
J3	Water
K	BUSINESS DEVELOPMENT
L	MANAGEMENT/ADMINISTRATION FEES
L1	Office staff
L2	Office services
L3	Temporaries
M	MEALS AND ENTERTAINMENT
M1	Meals/entertainment
M2	Food, non-restaurant entertainment
M3	Gifts
M4	Liquor
M5	Other entertainment expenses
M6	Tips/gratuities
N	MOTOR VEHICLE EXPENSES
N1	Insurance
N2	Maintenance
N3	Fuel and fluids
N4	Registration
N5	Auto lease
O	OFFICE EXPENSES
O0	Electric\onic equipment
O1	Photocopying
O2	Postage, courier
O3	Stationery, office supplies
O4	Telefax line rental
O5	Telefax toll charges
O6	Telephone line rental
O7	Telephone toll charges

P	RENT
Q	RESEARCH
Q1	Books/subscriptions
Q2	Database searches
Q3	Publications, cash purchases
Q4	Research fees
Q5	Other
Q6	Training/professional development
S	TRAVELLING EXPENSES
S1	Fares
S2	Hotels
S3	Meals and entertainment
S4	Per diem/cash expenditures
S5	Tolls/ferries
S6	Travel insurance
S7	Vehicle rentals
S8	Other
S9	Tips/gratuities
T	ALLOWABLE RESERVES
U	OTHER EXPENSES/PETTY CASH
U1	Public transit
U2	Parking meters
U3	Parking, receipted
U4	Taxis
U5	Pay phones
V	EQUIPMENT MAINTENANCE
V1	Parts
V2	Labor
W	CAPITAL ACQUISITIONS

This is only one example. Each service business, and each retail business, has expenses particular to those businesses, with emphasis on some. A florist's shop would have large and numerous expenditures for flowers, a bicycle repair shop would spend heavily on a basic parts inventory. A client of mine, a writer who uses temps to type his manuscripts and revisions, told me his biggest business expense is the cost of finding information. The specific costs of any particular business, though, are just a small part of the overall picture; the general costs required to keep a business, any business, going, are a bigger part of the picture, and generic.

The best thing to do, if you're confused about what fits as 'industry standard expenses' in your business, is to check if there's a Revenue Canada interpretation bulletin, circular, or other guides about the business. Check with an accountant. Find out if there are trade or professional associations for your businesses or professions, and see if they have tax issues committees, or information on tax issues unique to your business, and do what's necessary to acquire the information. This usually means joining the association. Join even if they don't have tax committees. The cost is a tax-deductible expense, and you'll be hooked into a good source of general information about your industry, and be able to mix with people with common concerns.

My first year, I even prepared my own income and expense statement, just so I would know what went into making one, to get a feel for what it represents. You have a sample of the income and expense statement in the handout.

	matching people with tasks
SKILLS	101 Rue Morgue Avenue
ON	Anytown, Ontario
DEMAND	Canada K1A 4M5
	(905) 123-4567 Fax: (905) 123-4577

INCOME AND EXPENSE STATEMENT 199___
INCOME

1)	Client A	$ _____		
2)	Client B	_____		
3)	Client C	_____		
4)	Client D	_____		
5)	Client E	_____		
6)	Client F	_____		
7)	Client G	_____		
8)	Client H	_____		
	INCOME TOTAL	_____	$_____	1

EXPENSES

ACCOUNTING, LEGAL, COLLECTION, CONSULTING
1) Eagle, Beagle, Blah, Lawyers
    301 Stornoway Road
    Anytown, Ontario $ _____ $ _____

ADVERTISING, PROMOTION
1) Meals $ _____
2) Liquor   _____
3) Gifts   _____
4) Food, Non-Restaurant   _____
5) Advertising   _____
6) Promotions   _____
    Total   _____ $ _____

AUTOMOBILE (Vehicle leased.
Costs based on XX per cent logged business use.)
1) Insurance $ _____
2) Maintenance   _____
3) Gas/Oil/Fluids   _____
4) Registration   _____
5) Lease 12 x _____ =   _____
    Total x XX%   _____ $ _____

CONVENTION EXPENSES $ _____

EQUIPMENT RENTAL $ _____

INSURANCE $ _____

INTEREST, BANK CHARGES
1) Loan Interest $ _____
2) Bank Charges   _____
    Total   _____ $ _____

LIGHT, HEAT, WATER

1) Water $ _____
2) Electricity   _____
3) Natural Gas   _____
   Total   _____ $ _____

MAINTENANCE
AND REPAIRS $ _____

MANAGEMENT AND
ADMINISTRATION FEES $ _____

OFFICE EXPENSES

1) Postage/Courier $ _____
2) Photocopying   _____
3) Office Supplies   _____
4) Books, Newspapers,
   Periodicals, Subscriptions   _____
5) Other Research Costs   _____
6) Phone Line and Tolls   _____
7) Fax Line and Tolls   _____
8) Office Services   _____
   Total   _____ $ _____

RENT $ _____

FEES (Contractors) $ _____

SALARIES/WAGES (Employees) $ _____

BENEFITS

1) Unemployment
   Insurance $ _____
2) Pension Plans   _____
3) Workers' Compensation   _____
4) Other   _____
   Total   _____ $ _____

TRAVEL EXPENSES

1) Air Travel $ _____
   A) Fares   (_____)
   B) Insurance (_____)
2) Meals on Research Trips   _____
3) Per Diem/Cash Expenses   _____
4) Project Expense   _____
5) Tolls/Ferries   _____
6) Accommodations   _____
7) Car Rentals   _____
   Total   _____ $ _____

OTHER EXPENSES

1) Taxis/Buses $ _____
2) Public Transit   _____
3) Parking, Metered
   and Receipted   _____
4) Public Phones   _____
   Total   _____ $ _____
   EXPENSES TOTAL $ _____ 2

CAPITAL COSTS

1) Office Furniture and Equipment
   Total x 20% Class 8 = $ _____
2) Computer and Printer
   Total x 30% Class 10 =   _____
   CAPITAL COSTS TOTAL   _____ $ _____ 3

PROFIT (LOSS) AT YEAR END 19___ (1-2-3) $ _____

My accountant, who works with all sorts of small business operators, used it as the basis of my audited statements and for my tax, and he said it was an excellent effort—he wished all his clients were that organized. The key issue he was referring to is the client always having information on file and under control. So, if you take away any ideas from the Oswego program, or this conference, I think the most important point is to keep timely, accurate records.

You see, I have no problems about paying for my accountant's time, because I use very little of it, and what I do use, I use efficiently. When I walk into her office, I have a file of organized information, and an agenda. Whether we're running one-person, home-based businesses, or national retail chains like the one Kevin built, keeping records is a discipline we would all do well to adopt, simply because any discipline we have, or can acquire, and use, makes us better businesspeople—it requires us to think in a measured, orderly fashion.

Most of us here who have gone into business know by now Kevin wasn't exaggerating when he called our tax system a horrible mess. We've learned, or are integrating with soul-stirring certainty, that there's no point complaining about it, because the policymakers aren't taking what we say seriously. Their thinking, tax and bureaucratic support systems are geared to a nation of job holders, and they have trouble knowing how to make the adjustments necessary to give businesspeople better and more chances at creating business success. So, I just hold my bitching to a minimum and ensure I keep, or effectively deploy to my benefit, as much of what I earn as possible, within the limits of existing law.

That's why I suggested all my temps register for GST numbers when the Goods and Sales Tax was introduced in 1991, even though the federal government didn't pay the registrants a fee to do the collecting, like the Ontario government does with provincial sales tax collections. I think that would have been a reasonable courtesy to the business community, you understand, because it does cost us to act as tax collectors.

Anyway, I recommended the temps register, when they asked for my advice, and I recommended they keep up their registrations as long as the government had the GST in place, or the other generalized value-added sales tax formulas they've attempted. At first I thought if Revenue Canada didn't require businesses with revenues under $30,000 per year to register, don't! Save the time and paperwork. Then I read further in the guidelines that non-registrants couldn't claim the tax they paid on purchases, what's called input costs. So, if in 1992 you earned $28,500, and had $15,000 in expenses on which you paid 7 per cent federal sales tax, you paid out $1,050 you could not claim. In essence, you voluntarily increased your overhead by 7 per cent, a cost that was recoverable had you registered. Look at it graphically on the last sheet of the handout.

HOW NOT REGISTERING FOR GST ADDED TO OVERHEAD

Example based on $1,000 in earnings

	Registered	Non-Registered
Gross Revenue Collected	$ 1,070	$ 1,000
Less: GST Remitted	70	–
	$ 1,000	$ 1,000
Expenses $107		107
Less: GST recovered 7 =	100	–
	$ 900	$ 893
GST collected and remitted	$ 70	
Less: GST recovered	7	
Net GST remitted	$ 63	

Once I realized what the impact of all this meant, I paid close attention to the sales tax debates—or at least asked my accountant to. She kept me current on developments, and as the government changed the rules of the sales tax situation, I adjusted my planning and management practices accordingly. The key is to stay informed and act, legally, in your best interests.

Another regular business practice to adopt is using project or work agreements if you're in service businesses. Invoices, statements and the like will make your lives easier, because these documents provide a paper trail and written record of transactions and terms everyone agreed to. Should disagreements happen, or the person who commissioned a project move on, and someone else takes over administration of the project, there's always a reference point. Then, as the project or work progresses, you can invoice the clients for work done, expenses they agree to cover, and everything is documented to their satisfaction, and yours.

KEVIN SHORT, PANEL MODERATOR: Can I cut in here, Anne?

ANNE PORTER: Sure.

KEVIN SHORT: In the case of a retail business, the paperwork going out is simpler, but the internal paper mill can become a nightmare if you don't organize yourself effectively before you start. By the time we had A Chip Five going, we were planning as far ahead as Chip 10, but we had to slow down, because we didn't have the systems in place to handle reporting from the five stores. We contracted with an independent accounting firm to set up a modular system to manage the financial paper flow on up to 20 stores, which could be increased in increments of five. So take the time at the front end to learn an effective way to organize your paper flow, then organize yourself to manage it.

ANNE PORTER: Thank you, Kevin. Now here's one more thing that's a part of paperwork, that most people don't understand is paperwork. During one of our sessions, Kieron Short dropped in for one of his random visits to the incubator classes. Kevin asked him to help with one of those tough questions we had thrown at him, and he decided we needed one of those 'cultural and historical perspectives on business in Canada' answers he so loves to include in his 'build for yourself a world-view' lectures.

(LAUGHTER)

That's when I found out Kieron had been trained as a lawyer, and he had come to the college principal's job from the McGill law faculty. I guess I loved the Oswego program because it helped me see how important it is to learn new things every day, in ways that make me feel smarter. The faculty, the other students, everyone encouraged me, and challenged me. I walked away from classes with them feeling smarter, and have done everything possible since then to spend more time with people like that.

Anyway, Kieron explained we in Canada have to recognize that a good part of our cultural heritage and most of our systems of law are legacies of our British colonial past. The principal feature of those legacies that stamps our national character is that everything starts as the property of the Crown (the government), and everything we, individual citizens, have is *by right* (permission or grant) of the Crown, including (especially!) our property and wealth, and even things we create and build. We are protected, however, by a series of important documents, laws, conventions and practices developed over hundreds of years to guarantee us all due process and rights against arbitrary treatment.

However, we had come up against the question of protecting ideas and inventions and the like. Paul Burnham had used the example of the better mousetrap, and wanted to know how far the government will go to protect an idea and patents from thieves.

That's when we learned the government *will not make one little move to protect an idea,* because ideas can't be patented, trademarked, or copyrighted. Even if they could be, the government's only part in protecting what is called intellectual property is to register your claim to having invented, written, recorded, or named it, as of a given day.

Ultimately, you and only you are responsible for protecting your rights. You have to get your idea or product to market as quickly as you can, and exploit it as aggressively as you can. If someone decides it's a nice piece and takes it to Hong Kong for reverse engineering and produces a knock-off, you have to hire the detectives and lawyers to search out the perpetrators, have them arrested and prosecuted, or sue directly for damages.

We were devastated to hear this, more so when Kieron told us that all the big name producers, Hermes, Rolex, Gucci, and a list of other names with immediate product-recognition value, spend millions on protecting their products and names. Failure to do so results in things like Xerox becoming xerox to describe a photocopy, even if it's done on a Canon machine.

CHAPTER NINE

The Fax, and Only the Fax

1995: *The Conference, Day One, A Banquet Hall*

"Last year, I took a trip with a fellow who asked me to participate with him in a business opportunity he was pitching," Kevin said, leaning into the speaker's lectern at the side of the head table. A large screen hung from the ceiling behind the table. "I took along a video camera, and I took some motion pictures, which I decided to use as illustrations for tonight's talk. One of the illustrations of the talk isn't the pictures themselves, but how they're presented."

Kevin pointed to a large box suspended from the ceiling. "That's a three-lens projection TV. It's connected to a computer. The videotape was fed into the computer, edited, some images were even set up as still photos, and mixed...with music, sound effects, dialogue, voice-over narration, and the whole thing is cued to my talk," he beamed at the diners. "*Technology*. It made my fortune as the product I sold and serviced, but, as a tool in the hands of people who are comfortable with it, technology can be used to leap tall buildings, save people in distress, and make fortunes."

He punched a button on the console next to him and nodded to the young man at the light dimmers.

"So kick back and relax, and take a little trip with me, and I'll show you ways to use technology, without becoming its prisoner," he said as the lights dimmed. "Come, fly with me..."

The screen filled with a shot, taken from the back seat of a helicopter, of the pilot against the backdrop of the Rocky Mountains seen through the windscreen.

"We'll be arriving in five minutes," the pilot said, his voice just audible in the odd echo-chambered effect unique to aircraft headset communications. Overhead, the rotor thwupped away, beating out its own soundtrack to the surreal sense of being suspended in mid-air that is characteristic of flying in a small helicopter. The chopper, a four seater being piloted into the Canadian Rockies near Banff, Alberta, also had an expensive movie camera mounted in a one-meter-diameter pod attached to its side. A cameraman in the passenger seat operated the camera by remote control.

NARRATOR: Ted Georgealidis is an Ottawa native in his early forties, who, in 1981, after already flying for about 10 years, set himself the goal of travelling as much of the world as he could, while flying, and getting paid to do both. By early '94, Ted had flown over large parts of North America, and had operating bases in Vancouver, in the Rockies just outside Banff National Park, and Los Angeles. He had also become one of five pilots on the North American movie industry's A-list, the 'preferreds' to be called when a shoot needed aerial photography, and was cutting what he would only describe as a comfortable six-figure income into the bargain.

This day in January '95, a few weeks after returning from a long trip to China to set up and co-ordinate a three-chopper feature-film shoot, Ted is flying for an ice beer commercial, the one where a long, slow shot closes in on an icy mountainside, and what looks like a brightly colored ant moving up its side.

The commercial was cut into the video. The shot tightened on a climber clawing and clambering his way over rock and ice, and a deep voice contemplated the wisdom of the ages, challenge and how both relate to beer. Then the shot closed in on a climber working his way up the peak. The triumph of imagery.

NARRATOR: The base for the shoot was a helipad at Dead Man's Flats, a tiny service community about 20 kilometres from the Banff National Park gates. The director and the rest of the crew, housed in Banff for the shoot, already had the ground support in place, and were waiting for the chopper to touch down. As soon as the engine was switched off, Ted was out of the pilot's seat. He pulled a small electronic organizer from his pocket and entered the flying time into the custom time log program that tracked his time in the air...for billing purposes. He checked in with everyone on the ground, the director, producer, production manager, his ground crew, and had the tanks topped up.

Then, while everyone else milled around in the modestly controlled confusion of the start of a shoot, Ted pulled a cellular phone out of his pocket, and took care of business. He retrieved the first messages of the day, and paced the helipad, responding feverishly to demands for his time.

Punch the keypad. Talk. Punch. Talk. He discusses the project he is on, the demands of other clients, the additional aviation fuel he needs delivered to the pad that day, not tomorrow. During one call he learns the new, revolutionary nose-camera mount for the second chopper booked for tomorrow hasn't been inspected yet by anyone from the Department of Transport, despite promises it would be. On the next call, he learns maybe it doesn't have to be checked, because someone has found a regulation to that effect. Then he finds out the British clients eager to shoot in the Rockies, who had booked his time for two days hence, are a day early, overlapping their shoot with the existing shoot. He takes a fourth call: Other clients want him in New Mexico in a few days.

NARRATOR: When he was done on the cellular, Ted pulled a laptop computer from his flight bag and wrote notes on the conversations, and a fax he would send out by fax/modem that afternoon from a nearby motel where he usually housed his ground crews while on a shoot. He and the manager had become friends when Ted ran a heli-skiing and general purpose flying service from the Flats in the late '70s and '80s, until the film business got him exclusively about 1989. The motel people and Ted still do each other little favors. Even that won't last.

"I'm researching the systems I can use to link the fax\modem in my laptop to the cellular," Ted says to the camera. "But what's available is too bulky and heavy for my needs, and a little too pricey for what you get."

NARRATOR: Ted would have looked harried at the shoot, except he was loving every minute of his high-paced morning. He has commanded small fleets of helicopters and light planes for shoots, and he's been hatching an idea about a flying movie, and every phone call means more work, more flying time, small steps closer to his dream aerial film.

Ted is without question a man who enjoys his toys and has figured out how to use them for maximum efficiency in helping him achieve his goals.

155

"The film industry is all hurry up and wait," he explains. "People ask for quotes for a job, then they go back and work with their budgets, then want me yesterday," he laughs. "And when they call, I want to be there, or available within a few minutes of the call."

NARRATOR: The price of not being easily available is that potential clients will just go on down the A list, and, if no one on that list is available, the B list cuts in.

"This is my connection to the world," Ted says, holding up his cellular phone. "The only problem is it changes your life. You're never alone, you never have any privacy, wherever you go."

NARRATOR: Ted has turned staying in touch, a key to his business, into an art, through a sophisticated understanding of what technology can do for him. He's also developed some attitudes to ensure technology serves him, not the other way around. That's the challenge most people in business for themselves have to face, because technology can free us from routine, having to manage large staff complements, and, for those in service and information-based businesses that don't require fixed places of business, technology gives us the freedom to roam and use 'virtual offices'. Equipped with laptop computers, fax\modems and cellular phones, we can do business from anywhere. Like Ted.

The video stopped on a still shot of Ted, holding up his cellular phone. The screen went dark, and the lights came up brightly around Kevin, but remained dim in the rest of the hall.

"Because we live with the sights and sounds of computers and fax machines and digital communications, we take them for granted," Kevin said. "But do you remember life at the beginning of the '80s?

"If you were one of the techno-pioneers, and had an answering machine with remote access, you had a base unit the size of one of today's laptop computers, and twice its weight. The remote control was a bulky, balky, and none-too-reliable unit the size of those old flip-top cigarette packs, at a discount price of $250. Today, a smaller, more efficient machine, with more features, and remote functions accessible from a phone's keypad, will set you back a whole 50, maybe 60 bucks at a discount electronics superstore. And it's reliable.

"Desktop computers were the stuff of science fiction in 1980, and, by 1982, they were high-end, exotic consumer fantasies pursued by the people we would end up calling hackers," Kevin said. "Trust me, I know," he chuckled and the audience laughed with him.

"Desktops were yet to make their mark as business tools, but anyone with imagination watching a typist work on a word processing machine with a control unit that looked as big as a Volkswagen Beetle, could see the future, especially if the observation was accompanied by a 'What if...?' about accounting, or data processing, or mailings.

"A machine we called a portable in 1983, became a luggable, then a doorstop when it soon became obsolete," Kevin said. "It weighed in at about 40 pounds, had two 64 kilobyte-capacity floppy drives, and cost about $2,500. A comparable unit today would be one of those little pocket organizers that costs about $250.

"Fax machines as we knew them were unreliable mechanical things that took forever to transmit information photographically. They were expensive, and people preferred to wait for couriers or the mail to deliver information rather than risk going blind trying to read a photofax. When digital faxes first came out, they were expensive and fickle, and it was more sensible to lease them, with service contracts, than buy. Now, you can get a basic free-standing fax machine for about $500, or a high-speed fax\modem board for your computer in the $200-250 range.

"The costs for technology keep dropping though, as yesterday's innovation becomes today's standard cleared out at deep discount prices when it becomes tomorrow's old technology.

"Consider the computer again, but not too much—the headaches aren't worth the return unless you sell computers, or write or publish software. If your most recent acquaintanceship with a computer was in a job, chances are you never had to worry about what was, or went on, inside it, except that it didn't lose your data. This is a reasonable position, more so when you're self employed, and you use the computer as a business tool. You just want to put the key in the ignition, switch it on and make it work.

"However, as a self-employed person, you're the boss, the handyman, the sweeper and file clerk, the comptroller and the purchasing department. You select the computer system to support your business operations. If you're like Ted, you will have been using computers in your business for a number of years, and will be comfortable buying your technology at reasonable prices.

"If not, try to avoid becoming part of the most interesting of observable phenomena resulting from the white-collar job purges of recent memory, the newly minted unemployed individual who saw the future, and it was self-employment using computer technology to create personal wealth. Because everyone, all the ads, and people at trade shows say the wave of future business is knowledge business, and computers are the access points to the knowledge base—the digital cabriolets scooting along the information superhighway, as it were—this pilgrim to the altar of technology spends a good piece of change on a computer and peripherals, then says, 'Well, I have my computer and stuff. I'm in business now, world.' Then looks around, bewildered, shaken, and terrified, and asks, 'What do I do now?'

"What indeed? It's analogous to the situation Laura Gunderson, the career planning consultant, has witnessed since 1989, when the big corporate purges began happening in Toronto. People would go out and spend heavily on image—cards, letterheads, logos, brochures—*without even finding out if there was a market demand for the goods or services they offered.* Essentially, technology can start as a self-employed person's security blanket and quickly become a psychological leg-hold trap," Kevin said, as the lights around him dimmed and the screen lit up with a photo he had staged with an actor, looking harried, surrounded by a pile of smashed up old computers. "It's a jagged circle of thinking. 'I need technology to succeed. I have all this expensive technology. I'm working to pay for the technology. The technology is obsolete. I have to upgrade because I need state-of-the art technology to succeed. I have all this expensive technology.'"

There were three sounds, like loud, heavy sighs, and confetti and streamers floated down on the diners to their delighted 'oohs' and 'aahs'. They looked up, and indoor fireworks went off, shooting brilliant orbs of flashing, hissing light around the room. Then cold, silver-blue sparkling showers of light streamed from the floral centrepieces on each table.

"Some of you will remember Daniel Best, of AirCare Products, whose daughter nicknamed him The Pyro Guy. He's the fellow who wanted to sell confetti cannon, but found the whole range of special effects and pyrotechnics to be a better business bet?" There were cheers and applause from the audience. "That's his handiwork, folks—pretty, exciting, but a little risky, inherently dangerous. Yet he approached his first computer purchase in a state of near terror.

"There was so much he didn't know or understand. For a week, he took me to lunch and asked me about how the computer works, and the best way to deploy it. His work at the time, when he was doing technical production for live theatre and industrial shows, didn't require all the hallmarks of technology, or so he said, as he resisted the purchase. Then he admitted he was late buying computer equipment for his office, because every computerized lighting and effects system he was asked to work with failed shortly before or after the curtain went up.

"Just as an aside, folks, we ran a feasibility study to see if it was worth setting up a company to build systems that were reliable. But we found by then the market was already saturated.

"In his business, people would call up The Pyro Guy, tell him what they needed him to do. They'd agree on fees, and he would peck out a letter, and his invoice, on his old typewriter. When he moved into the pyrotechnics and special effects work, all that had to change. The business required a certain level of flash and sophistication, and efficient office technology, particularly the computer and a fax. He had to prepare bids, and detailed proposals.

"His accounting needs expanded continually for two years after he moved his books and billings onto computer. He began to write the copy for his own brochures and new product and new service circulars to his clients on the computer, and deliver them on disk to a printer who gives him high-quality output. Today, like the rest of us who were once bewildered by the machinery of business, he counts it as a tool, and can't understand how he got on without it.

"Now watch the screen closely, folks," Kevin prompted. A small explosive device went off under the screen, smoke billowed in front of it, then dissipated. On screen, a tall, thin bespectacled man sat in an office chair, facing the camera. A computer screen could be seen just over his shoulder. It was dark, except for a screen saver— little explosions, naturally. A line came up on the screen, identifying him as Daniel Best, The Pyro Guy.

"After using a pager for years, I got a cellular phone last year, and I was terrified," he said. "I had heard of people racking up thousands of dollars in bills on these things—" He held his phone up to the camera. "—but I didn't build up my business, or establish any prosperity by throwing money around. My concern wasn't the call charges themselves." He shrugged. "They're a cost of doing business. I just wanted to make sure they weren't frivolous costs, and, ensure, wherever possible, that they were money generators. I was also concerned about the intrusiveness on my life, which is already pretty busy."

There was a flash, smoke filled the screen, then disappeared. Best and the office were replaced with moving pictures of a busy commercial street filled with earnest-looking men and women talking into cellular phones as they walked along.

NARRATOR: So Daniel watched cellular users, and examined his service package and the features of the phone to figure out how to most efficiently and cost-effectively use the phone. Then he examined his patterns of incoming and outgoing calls from his office, and how he responded to his pager.

What he saw was that most people using a cellular respond to it in an almost Pavlovian manner. It rings. They answer. The charge timer starts ticking.

Daniel decided that rather than let the phone control him, he would control the phone. He disciplined himself not to answer automatically whenever he was out of the office, except when he was expecting a particular call. Otherwise, he would let the caller leave a message, which was one of the features in his service package. Then he would do a quick check for messages every hour, and place his calls, either from the cellular, a pay phone, or any other available phone. This way, he stayed efficient, and in control of his costs.

There was another flash on the screen, and Daniel reappeared.

"You see, I think sometimes the electronics—laptops, cellulars, fax\modems—are just toys and we get caught up playing catch-up to other people and their toys, and it all becomes just another expense," he said. "The key, I found, is meeting my needs, not some image fantasy, and making the phone a—" He seemed to grope for words, then shrugged and said, "—a profit centre."

. . . .

FROM THE TRANSCRIPT OF **MAKING FRIENDS WITH TECHNOLOGY,**
A PANEL DISCUSSION AND WORKSHOP AT THE 1995 OSWEGO
COLLEGE SELF-EMPLOYMENT CONFERENCE *(Available from Allied Tape
and Transcription Services Ltd., c/o Oswego College, $7.50 a copy, sales taxes included.)*

SUSAN MANYFINGERS: Making technology work for us isn't that hard, as long as we don't go looking for the monster in the box. I know it's there, it took me prisoner for a week when I was in Copenhagen working with a gallery to set up a distribution deal for native art. I travel a great deal in my work, and have a staff of one back home in Calgary who runs the office. We like to stay in touch, and find it cheaper to send each other faxes than talk on the phone.

Have any of you made the comparisons? You can get more information across clearly in a two-page fax that takes two minutes to transmit than you can in a 10-minute phone conversation.

So I travel with a laptop computer that has a fax\modem. I compose my faxes and just send them out. Except, that week in Copenhagen, I felt trapped, because I couldn't send stuff directly from the computer over the phone lines. I had to print the faxes out and send them on the gallery's machine.

That's a minor irritant, though. You won't know how easily you can develop a computer dependency until you have lost a week's worth of work to the ozone, and your backups are two days old. Grown men have been known to bawl like babies in this situation, and vow never again to offend the Great God Backup by not making daily offerings. Ultimately, the task is to figure out how a pricey mess of plastic, metal, and wires that are just incomprehensible voodoo to most of us, can make us money, or at least cut down the costs of making money, and generally make us more efficient.

The first step is to understand that each program has a learning curve. At the beginning, a new program will be a great mystery, but persevere. Don't fall into the trap of only reading the manual *when all else fails.* Unfortunately, the manufacturer's manual will read like gibberish, because there seems to be a law in computer manual writing that condemns to some kind of purgatory people who make them intelligible. Often it happens that third-party manuals, written by literate people who use the programs, range from much better to superior. For example, WordPerfect is a wonderful word processing program, with an incredibly complicated manufacturer's manual. For years, a company called Que has published excellent manuals that put the ones provided by the software publisher to shame.

Don't feel bad and beat yourself up for being six kinds of idiot because you can't decipher computer manuals. Kevin told me once about a geophysicist he knows whose profession teaches him to always read the manual first. He uses complex scientific equipment and computer technology to find oil hundreds of feet underground, yet he has been known to mutter many a curse about software manual writers who can't keep things simple. Mention Windows to him, and you can hear his teeth grind, and see knots form in his forehead. He is almost taking it as a personal affront that he has to take a Windows course to learn how to make the $%^&@* thing run.

It helps somewhat that the more complex and costly programs have toll-free customer assistance numbers to call. Actually, that's why they're so expensive, but the service also builds their reputations. A rule of thumb to observe here is that the cheaper the software, the more expensive the service support will be. Buyer beware!

Kevin gave us strong counsel on staying sane when buying computer equipment and software. Who better to tell us these things than the guy who created A Chip Off The Old Block? I finally have an answer to that question: Me! One of his students, a technophobe who listened closely, took his advice and compiled for herself a list of guidelines for using technology effectively. It's in the handout for this workshop.

SUSAN MANYFINGERS' 10 COMMANDMENTS
FOR USING TECHNOLOGY

1. FIRST LEARN ABOUT THE APPLICATIONS YOU WANT TO USE, LIKE WORD PROCESSING, ACCOUNTING, DESKTOP PUBLISHING, COMMUNICATIONS.
2. TEST DRIVE EVERYTHING TO FIND THE MOST EFFECTIVE COMBINATION OF HARDWARE AND SOFTWARE TOOLS.
3. THEN BUY AS MUCH POWER, SPEED AND MEMORY AS YOU CAN AFFORD.

The pace of change in the industry is so intense that the machinery you buy today is already obsolete when you take it out the door, and the software version you bought is not far behind.

You'll never stay on top of change, will barely pace change, and trying to do so is a sucker's game. So, instead, buy what will meet your present needs. Make sure you get the system seller to customize it with enough flexibility to adapt to change for as long as possible, because the biggest problem we consumers face with computer technology is the growth in program sizes and speed requirements. They eat up storage memory, operating memory and time, so that's why you want to buy as much speed, power and memory as you can afford.

4.   BUYING COMPUTERS FROM GENERAL-PRODUCT CONSUMER ELECTRONICS DISCOUNTERS CAN BE RISKY BUSINESS.

The fortunate among us never learn why this matters. Those who do, learn it the hard way. Kevin makes some distinctions though. He created a *specialty computer discounter* that offered full service to customers because he sold in enough volume to get discounts he could pass on to his customers. His prices were then cheap enough that a buyer could still purchase a service plan package that didn't seem to be an exorbitant extra cost.

If you buy computer hardware from a *general-product con-sumer electronics discounter,* particularly the central processing unit—the box—you'll get a price break, and maybe help loading the gear into your car. After that, you're on your own. The dis-counters hope never to see you again, except when you come in to buy more. But ask for after-sales service, and they'll try to sell you in-house extended warranties or special service packages, when all you want to know is how to connect your monitor, or set a switch on your printer.

If you buy from a *full-service computer retailer,* you likely won't get a great discount—though always ask for little extras, like free cables, or spare printer ribbons, inkjet reservoirs, anything, just ask—but you will be able to count on after-sales help in getting you set up and running, and a certain amount of phone support. House calls are rare unless the sales representative you work with also travels to offices to ensure efficient set-up. You can be assured the service costs are factored into the price. The key point is it's available. The second important point is that general-product consumer electronics discounters sell off-the-shelf packages; the specialty computer discounters can customize to your needs, for a price; the full-service retailers can customize to your needs for a higher price.

When it comes to certain peripherals like printers, modems and software, buying from discounters isn't a problem, though the slim profit margins and stiff competition in software sales mean the discount from discounters can't be that great. The key point here is that if you do buy software from a discounter, you still won't be left in the lurch. Many of the high-priced software publishers offer service support via toll-free help lines, and they can give better assistance than any sales or service representative.

5. PLAYING WITH BOOTLEG SOFTWARE IS A MUG'S GAME.

Software is property, no different than a car or a piece of jewelry—it belongs to someone. It's technically called intellectual property and ownership is covered by copyright, which is the grant from the sovereign power (the government) to a creator of the sole right to copy a written, musical or art work.

People all over the place use bootleg software, and every time they switch on the computer, they're breaking the law, the same way people break the law when they photocopy books or duplicate music tapes and CDs. Software publishers can't police the whole world, though they do spend small fortunes to protect their copyrights. There was also a spate of cases in the mid-'80s when large companies were caught with desktops full of bootleg software. They paid huge fines and had to purge their systems.

(Just as a digression, have you noticed how people justify using bootleg software because it's so much cheaper? It always strikes me as ironic that the people I've seen loading their computers with bootleg software are often the people who complain the most, loudest, and most bitterly over how you can't trust people out there, and the moment you bring a good idea to the market, someone's always trying to steal it, etc., etc.)

If cost bothers you, try a less expensive piece of software, or try shareware, often excellent programs available as undocumented or partially documented test programs for nominal fees of about $5 through electronics and software shops. You can try them, and, if you like them, send in a licence fee, for which your copy will be registered, you will get bound documentation, service support, and notice of upgrades.

Besides the 'do the right thing' angle, there's a pragmatic reason for not loading your system with bootleg software—it's the computer equivalent of unprotected sex in the '90s. Your chances of letting a computer virus loose in your system increase the more you put foreign disks in the drives. Enough said.

6.   BUY AS IF YOU WERE BUYING A CAR.

Don't let yourself be intimidated by computers, technospeak, or salespeople. Unlike auto salespeople, who don't often know a lot about cars, computer salespeople were shaken out a long time ago, and the technical illiterates were purged. Now, most computer salespeople know their technology. Some will bowl you over with their expertise, but remember, they are still trying to sell you something expensive.

Use all the buying savvy you would use for a car. If you have a friend who knows about computers, take him or her along, or at least get an explanation about what you ought to be looking for. There are also magazines and buying guides you can check for information. Whatever you do, negotiate for the best price. Your attempts might not be successful, but at least you will have tried.

7.   OBSERVE MAINTENANCE SCHEDULES, AND BACK UP FILES
     REGULARLY.

Kevin says his experience was that if a computer and peripherals made it through the first 30 days without a major breakdown, they'd give trouble-free service for a long time. When they're ready to give out, you'll note warning signs, like the pitch of the whine made by the hard drive will change, signalling a bearing is wearing out. You'll note odd errors in data sometimes, or a weird wavering on the monitor. The most impressive and painful sign of trouble is when you switch on the machine and nothing happens.

The biggest enemies of computer components are heat, humidity, dust and tobacco smoke. The critical problem is that the heat generated by the machine can result in tiny drops of condensation on electrical contacts, which attract dust and smoke particles that can gum up or corrode the contacts and cause problems. So a regular maintenance routine will save you trouble. If you have a desktop system, open it up every few months and blow out dust with a can of bottled air. Clean the floppy drives regularly, and dust the cabinetry. Always ensure

jacks, plugs, junctions are tight and secure. Dust your monitor
screen regularly. Clean your keyboard keys regularly—a bit of
rubbing alcohol on a Q-Tip will do wonders. And don't spill anything into your keyboard.

8. AVOID BUYING THE WHOLE-NUMBERED VERSION OF
    SOFTWARE, IF POSSIBLE.

The fellow who sells and maintains my computer calls this a computer user's superstition, but says it has enough history to back it
up. Software publishers identify their software by version
number. WordPerfect 5.1, DOS 6, then 6.2, that sort of number-
ing. When the number is a whole number, like 5.0, it's the first
release of new or upgraded software to hit the market. It has
been written and tested in the software development lab, test
groups, and focus groups, and the publisher hopes the glitches
and bugs have been worked out.

Well, let a million consumers get their hands on a new piece
of software, and they'll put demands on it the designers and
testers never dreamed of. Computer users are a curious and loud
lot—they let publishers know what they think of the product.
So, VERSION 5 comes out, then is upgraded to VERSION 5.3 six,
eight, maybe 10 months later. My computer guy says just try to
avoid the whole number versions of programs. He has proven
reliable enough, and saved me enough trouble already, that I
took his word and bought into his superstition.

9. CRY FOR THE PAPERLESS OFFICE.

It was a great idea when proposed: A desktop computer in every
office means we'll use less paper. Right, and the check is in the mail.

Acres of trees have been consumed in magazine stories and
doctoral theses about the truth or fallacy of that statement. What
appears to be the case is those who use computers, but were
brought up in the typewriter era, still need to put stuff on an
8½x11 inch piece of paper to 'see' it. (Or they're related to ger-
bils, and need lots of paper around them.) And the computer is
so co-operative about quick, easy printing of documents—forests
of them.

Those who grew up in the computer era tend to 'see' things
in terms of computer screens, and aren't as quick to punch the
print key.

Those who aspire to flexibility have found a reasonably effective middle ground and treat the computer like an electronic filing cabinet. Start by thinking economy and environmental friendliness; paper costs, and is made from our friends the trees.

If a document needs to be printed because it's going to be sent, faxed, mailed, or otherwise provided as hard copy to another individual, then print it, once. If you fax it, file the original, or recycle it immediately—a copy is in the computer—but just don't let the paper pile up.

The key idea here is the storage capacity of a computer is great, and you can always purge and copy files for archiving. This 'virtual file cabinet' will only work, though, if you develop the discipline to regularly back up your hard disk drive to a tape drive, or a packet of floppy disks. This way, if you do have a crash, you have a copy of the data to fall back on.

10. DON'T BUY ELECTRONIC TOYS JUST BECAUSE YOU
    THINK, OR EVERYBODY YOU KNOW TELLS YOU THAT
    YOU NEED THEM.

Not only is that the message for using technology, but also for the entire Oswego program. The best decisions you make are the ones that are informed by your needs, not by what other people tell you you should or should not need.

CHAPTER TEN

Everything is Negotiable

1995: *The Conference, Morning, Day Two*

Monique Pelletier left the breakfast buffet with a plate of fruit, and scanned the college dining room. She saw Kevin, and headed for the vacant chair at his table. Kevin rose when she arrived, and introduced Monique to the two people at the table she didn't know, his wife, Danielle Short, a petite dark-haired woman who carried herself as if she were six feet tall, and his daughter Rachel, a self-possessed, dark-haired, 10-year-old with a streak of mischief just looking for the right moments to appear.

"I have looked forward to meeting you, Danielle," Monique said with a smile. "Is it true, as Kevin says, that you are the architect of his success?"

Danielle smiled broadly at Monique, and fondly at Kevin. "I just contributed to a great idea that had nowhere to go but up."

"But those of us who have watched these two operate have witnessed a real partnership," Kieron said.

Kevin laughed. "Right. If we were one person, we'd be perfect."

"But perfection would be so boring," Danielle said. "It leaves so little to learn and experience."

"So are your parents perfect?" Monique asked Rachel.

"I don't know what perfect is," Rachel said turning to look at her father and mother. "They just negotiate a lot."

"Excuse me?" Monique said, perplexed.

"Well, in general, human beings lead healthy, successful lives when we live them by commitment. We commit to ideas, people, buying a car," Kevin explained. "But, if we don't know what is required to fulfil a commitment, or what we are committing to, commitment is hard to make and meet. So, we—Danielle and I—learned to establish ground rules together—"

"Boundaries," Brenda suggested.

Danielle nodded. "Boundaries," she agreed.

"—rules we negotiate and base on our values. Then we work to stick to them," Kevin said. "Or renegotiate, as necessary."

"I just think Mom and Dad like to talk with each other, because they always have their heads together, discussing things," Rachel said. "They include me in a lot of discussions, but they still make the decisions."

"When you're old enough, you get full voting rights," Kevin said.

"That's why I need a brother," she pouted. "Then there will come a day when I don't have to worry about being outvoted."

Kevin laughed, and fondly rubbed his daughter's back.

"You used to do that to make me go to sleep," Rachel said.

"I can only hope..." he laughed.

"That's why we negotiate everything," Danielle said. "It's a contract in our home."

"Contract?" Monique asked.

Kevin nodded. "The best way to teach is by example. The best example is ritual, as long as it doesn't become rigid, and ritual for its own sake." He looked at his wife. "You want to start?"

"Rule number one," Danielle said. "*We work not to assume, nor take for granted anything about ourselves, each other, or the values we hold.*"

"Rule number two," Rachel said. "*Everything is negotiable.*"

"Rule number three," Kevin said. "*Negotiate everything.*"

"Or *at least try*," Rachel added. "I don't always get what I want, but Mom and Dad want me to know that anything is possible."

"Excuse me, but did you put Rachel through your program?" Jimmy Baldwin asked.

"Sounds like it," Kieron laughed. "I've seen some of the sessions Kevin has run."

"Now, Kieron, would you have us involved with your program if we didn't practise what we preach?" Danielle asked.

"Are you kidding? You don't know how thrilled I was when I sat in on the first class you two taught together, and saw how you work," Kieron smiled.

She looked at him for a moment, then her face lightened up when she remembered. "The business, partners, and negotiating session?"

Kieron nodded.

"That's an odd combination of topics," Jimmy said.

"Not really," Danielle said. "Not if you operate from the principle that all business transactions occur within relationships we establish, and are really exercises in managing options, which is what negotiating is about—*arriving at options that serve the needs of all the people involved...*"

. . . .

1990: *A Seminar Room at Oswego College*

"Kevin, how do you buy wholesale?" Brenda asked.

Kevin stared at Brenda. When he was growing up, he watched his father go from working a pharmacy with retail sales to running a wholesale operation, when he set up and ran the service centre for the Central Drugs co-op. He heard his parents talk about business at the dinner table in the same conversations that broached health, politics and whatever was the important topic of the day. Even Tony, the tough Sicilian who drove the centre's first delivery truck, then ran the fleet and retired as manager of the warehouse, talked about business when Kevin accompanied him on his rounds, after school.

Doing business, buying, selling, were a reality Kevin experienced and saw in action daily, from an early age until his late teens. The idea of buying wholesale (cheap) and selling retail (dear), for the profit in between, was the foundation and focus of his business philosophy, and it was a habit of mind to ask, "What trail does the buck follow to get to me?" So, when Brenda asked the question, he realized he had assumed everyone knew what wholesale meant, and those who were in business, or going into it, knew how to buy from producers or their agents in the distribution system.

In fact, he had always thought everyone knew the primary rule of commerce—buy low and sell dear—until he had seen people fight for places in line, afraid they wouldn't be able to buy gold, as a hedge, or for profit, in '81, when gold prices ran up to the US$800 range. If people wanted to speculate on gold, they should have bought before the price run-up, Kevin had reasoned. But then, no one had expected gold, which had languished in the US$300 range for years, would appreciate so quickly, he countered. But then, again, he argued, the time to buy something like gold is when no one wants it, when money is cheap and easy to acquire. Then a person just had to be able to think of the money as spent and unrecoverable, and be pleasantly surprised when it proved to be worth more, when all other prices rose, or to have held its value when all others fell.

Anyway, gold and people's buying habits notwithstanding, this was the first time anyone had ever asked him the question, so Kevin shrugged, and said, "Simple. Call the supplier you want to deal with. Explain what you want. Cut a deal."

Brenda said, "I was researching the feasibility of an on-hold business, for the potential service business report—"

Kevin shook his head, and held up his hand. "On-hold business?"

"You know, when you call someone and the receptionist puts you on hold, and you hear a radio station?" Brenda asked. "That's 'on hold', and a new twist—not ours, it's already being done—is to replace the radio signal with voice ads that feature the business's products or services, or that week's special."

"Can a person make a living at it?" Kevin asked.

"If I could find out wholesale prices for the cassette machine I would have to wire into the client's phone system, I could finish the spreadsheet and get some projections," she said. "But when I call distributors for price quotes, they send me to their retail clients, who charge full retail price, or might give me a discount on retail."

"Did you speak to sales reps, or sales managers?"

"Sales reps," she replied glumly.

"Well, don't give up," Kevin said. "Just move up the decision-making ladder. Reps are gatekeepers, with limited authority to say yes, which leaves them little to do except take your orders, or say no."

"So...?" Brenda grumbled.

"So, speak to the next person in the pecking order, and keep moving up and talking until you get satisfaction," he said. "Let them know you're a reseller, just like their other retail clients, not an end user, and you want wholesale prices."

The room was silent as Brenda digested these ideas. She was wrestling with the mental resistance change often triggers, because we process new information autobiographically—through the screens of our experience and comfort zones. Without an intellectual, emotional, or physical contact point with an event, or a concept, people dig in and fall on their 'buts'…into the security of habit.

"You mean talk to the sales manager?" she finally said.

"Or the branch manager, or the regional sales manager. Or the national sales manager. Or the president of the company, if that's what it takes," Kevin said. "And if that doesn't help, hit other distributors."

"But I'm in start-up," she objected. "I won't be buying in quantities…"

"And you never will, if you keep thinking that way," Kevin said. "You have the principle down: *Keep your quality as high as possible while using every means to keep down the unit cost to supply the client.* Now, make it work."

"Right. I want better operating margins, so I have the leeway to offer clients package deals, and get them to commit to contracts in increments of three months," Brenda said. "I figured that part out myself," she added proudly. "Discount my unit profit margins enough for the customer to buy in volume, and, ultimately, my profit will be better, because I'll be spending less time developing clients and sales leads, and more time selling more product to regular clients on an ongoing basis."

"Excellent! Are you sure you haven't been in sales before?" Kevin asked.

"No," Brenda laughed. "I've just worked with numbers, and listened to you for the last few months."

"Bravo. Keep it up," Kevin said. He turned to the rest of the class. "Brenda's principle is a good one. Keep it in mind, because any of you could be in this position. You would have to make the case to the wholesaler that it's in his or her interest to supply you."

Danielle had come to conduct the session with Kevin that morning, and she volunteered a suggestion: "Try an approach like: 'I'm a reseller. I'm selling the product into a market niche it hasn't been used for before, which offers you broader exposure to a business clientele without spending extra advertising or promotional dollars. I'll be increasing your sales and market penetration.'" She looked at Brenda. "The key is to position the benefits of dealing with you in the distributor's mind."

"All that to buy wholesale? The cost in time of getting a price break could kill the advantage of the break," John Tan suggested.

"Maybe," Kevin agreed half-heartedly. "But when you're deciding if the price break compensates for the time you expend to find it, you have to factor in the long-term benefit of establishing the arrangement once, then maintaining it with your supplier."

"You must understand that Kevin believes success, in any venture in any aspect of life, is a half beat past the point where most people give up," Danielle said.

"That's true," Kevin nodded. "Success is a bit like that item you misplaced, and you find it in the last place you would have looked for it. Well, it *was* the *last* place you looked."

"This comes under the gospel according to Kevin," Danielle laughed. "Everything is negotiable. Fortunately, I bought into the idea early. It contributed greatly to making our marriage work, and making A Chip work." She paused a moment, then a shocked look crossed her face. "I just realized how that sounds without background, because if everything in life is negotiable, then nothing is of value, and that's the furthest thing from the way we operate."

"Thank you, Danielle," Kevin whispered.

"There has to be a baseline of value and values beyond which each individual in a transaction, or relationship, won't go," Danielle said. "In the business context, I once watched a fellow try to negotiate with Kevin for a better price on a computer than Kevin could afford to give him. You remember, Mike—"

"Michael Hayakawa." Kevin nodded. "Mike had been born in Atlanta, Georgia, and took great delight at the reactions his accent got him. That guy needed the computer like you wouldn't believe," Kevin said. "That was for Expat Exploration and Drilling, a company he set up in Calgary."

"What was he doing there?" John asked.

"I asked him that once. He said, 'I trained as a geophysicist. The oilpatch is where the stuff I'm interested in is being done.'"

"How do you know all these people and their stories?" Susan demanded. "I've been dying to ask this for weeks."

"Kevin *has* told you his opening policy on new stores?" Danielle asked and looked around.

"He's told us a number," Mac said.

"He would spend between two and four days in each new store, every four weeks for the first few months, just to monitor operations," Danielle said.

"Haven't heard that one," John said.

"Well, he met a lot of people, and he has this natural curiosity that has him always asking them questions about themselves and their work," Danielle said. "People respond when you ask about them, especially when they see you're genuinely interested in their answers." She paused. "Of course you also have to know how to end a conversation, without offending a person, so you can get back to work." Danielle paused to let the idea of contact, movement to closure, or disengagement roll around their minds for a while. "There's another reason for knowing how to cut off a conversation. When you start to look prosperous, people are always bringing you business deals to invest in."

Kevin nodded agreement. "And the ideas can go from crackpot to brilliant, but no one has enough money to invest in everything. Anyway, Mike is a geophysicist in his mid-fifties, and when I met him in '86, he was just starting to recover from the collapse of his independent oil exploration and consulting business following the global oil industry price clashes that occurred between 1981 and '83..."

Mike and his wife, Marie, a partner in Expat, had developed a recovery plan. The vehicle they chose to ride back to prosperity was a business opportunity that developed when the Canadian oil industry began shrinking its way back to profitability in the '80s.

The fully integrated oil companies, the majors, which had previously hired people in-house to do every job from finding the oil to delivering processed goods to private consumers, industry, and agriculture, decided they couldn't afford to do everything themselves any more, because high administrative overhead costs made the product unprofitable. So they rebuilt themselves through divestiture of old, uneconomical properties, and acquisition of newer, more efficiently drilled and exploited properties. They also pared down their assets to operate only their most profitable fields, to buy excess product from independent operators, or to finance oil deals—plays as they're called.

The trimming resulted in large-scale layoffs, and aggressive, experienced and talented oil finders, speculators and deal makers, young and old, hit the streets with enough money or credibility to cook up their own low-cost oil and gas plays, production from which the majors were always eager to buy. Mike's particular part of any deal was based on his ability to find places on the ground to point to, and say, "Drill here." For this, he would get fees, and an interest in each well that translated into royalties on sale of the gas and oil he found.

The problem facing the industry was that even so-called low-cost oil and natural gas were expensive to find and exploit. Mike, a scientist, took the scientist's route to solving a problem, and began to explore ways of finding hydrocarbon deposits at cheaper-than-conventional costs by using science more sophisticated than the traditional, expensive, and low-productivity geological and seismic surveying. He found his answer in a geophysics journal, and began developing the technology and how to apply it.

His only problem was he needed more powerful computer equipment to process the data, but no banking institution would write him a business loan for the computer equipment, because the size of the loan, and the interest they'd earn, didn't make it worth the effort of doing the paperwork. Then, because of his and Marie's financial ruin in the wake of the oil price crashes, no financial institution would give them a personal loan for the equipment, and no leasing company would touch the purchase.

"So he was trying to do a deal with me on the equipment," Kevin said. "And I wasn't insulted or annoyed that he wanted to wheel. I might not give in to the request to negotiate further, but I do honor people who at least ask."

"Yes, but then what happened—" Danielle had to stifle her laughter. "—was that Kevin invested money in Mike's company, some of which Mike used to buy the computer equipment he needed."

"Well, I was trained as an electrical engineer, so techno-freak to techno-freak, he posed an interesting enough solution that made sense," Kevin explained.

"I'm glad you invested. They've become good friends of our family," Danielle said.

"And he still wanted to dicker with me on the price," Kevin laughed. "But I'm still a proud shareholder in Expat Drilling and

Exploration Ltd., of Calgary, which receives royalties from 15 producing wells drilled using Mike's radiometric and magnetographic finding technology."

"And in a few years, we'll have parts of a whole field or two," Danielle said.

"That's positively Machiavellian," John said. "You won two ways in that transaction."

"We *both* won," Kevin said. "We found a way to trade value, and did it amicably because my counter-offer was do-able. Two parties. Win. Win."

"That's the key to successful negotiating," Danielle said.

"You see, most people think negotiating is going into a room and beating up on people," Kevin said. "If you're prepared to accept abuse, fine, go to it. Do business with those kinds of scuzzballs. I won't, because the abuse won't stop there, and I will not allow myself to be subjected to any kind of abuse."

"Your father taught you that?" Brenda asked.

"Him and a fellow named Herb Cohen," Kevin said.

"You can negotiate anything," Mac said.

"That's right," Kevin said to the perplexed looks the exchange triggered in the rest of the people in the class. "The book.... *You Can Negotiate Anything.* Cohen wrote it. He's a brilliant negotiator, and writes and lectures lucidly about the art. I have read and reread his book, listened to tapes of him talking about negotiating—"

"This was one of the strengths of A Chip," Danielle said. "Kevin established from the start the philosophy of constant learning and professional development."

"Hey, come on Danielle. Take credit for your share of the idea," Kevin chided her gently.

She smiled and shrugged. "Okay. I admit it. The teacher in me couldn't help but intercede when Kevin would moan about his inadequacies as a businessman, so I helped him shape the policy."

"And administered it brilliantly when she joined the company as an active participant," Kevin said.

Danielle smiled charmingly and took a small bow.

"Now, I learned three important lessons about negotiating from Cohen, *the first being that negotiations are just transactions between people, best concluded through reasonable discussion, usually by people* who are programmed to win," Kevin said. "Two: *My task in a negotiation is to keep my options, and my ability to act on them, as open as possible, while nailing down exactly what the other party's part is, including how his money finds its way into my pocket, and being aware the whole time that the other party is trying to do the same.* Three: *The success of the negotiation comes of knowing, before I enter negotiations, what I need out of the transaction, and the price I'm prepared to pay to get it. The rest is just process, and Cohen's good about explaining process.*"

"Which is what you're practising in your negotiating simulations," Danielle said to the class.

"Exactly, so let's go back to you, Brenda, doggedly searching out the right person to talk to so you can get a deal on cassette players," Kevin said. "Get off your 'but', that you're a start-up business, and won't be buying in large lots. Rather, know that you are worth something to the supplier as a client. Maybe not a great deal now, or on one big buy, but likely over time," Kevin suggested. "*You never know what you can get out of life until you ask for it.* Write that in your notebooks and think on it for a while after this session is over. Throw out the idea of a smaller price break on volume purchases over time, rather than a bigger break on a one-time, multi-unit purchase."

"Ummm, I'm not sure what you mean by that," Brenda said.

Danielle addressed her directly: "Say a distributor quotes you a wholesale price of $60 per unit. Chances are you're talking a gross wholesale—her best price to a low-volume buyer. You can bet there's a scale of price breaks, and a large retailer gets a better discount on 1,000 units, say an additional 30 per cent. Or, if not 30 per cent, payment terms of 50 per cent down, delivery in eight weeks, and final payment 90 days after delivery, no interest on the outstanding balance."

"Whoa!" Brenda exclaimed. "In the plan for this mythical company, I'm not looking at 1,000 units, and I don't have a lot of money to put into inventory."

"Of course not," Danielle agreed. "But assume you've targeted getting 60 new clients over the first three months, so you guarantee to buy 60 units over 90 days, in lots of 10, for an additional five per cent discount on gross wholesale for cash payment on each lot," Danielle said. "And you offer to defer the entire discount to the last lot of 10, so the total discount for the 60 units is deducted from the price of the last 10 units, only if you buy the last 10 units."

After another long pause, during which it was almost possible to hear Brenda's eyes roll up in her head—though she didn't go TILT!—she slowly said, "Oh, I see it. They're moving product, and into a new market. I get my price break, if I buy 60 within 90 days, and if I don't buy my 60, they still get their gross wholesale price, and I'll have operated on a realistic pricing structure while hustling for business. If I get my large-scale discount my profit margin improves. Everyone should be happy."

"You'll never know until you ask," Kevin said. "And *you'll never know what you can get until you exhaust the opportunities of asking* for what you need. So, remember, no matter what anyone says, *Everything is negotiable*, so *negotiate everything. Try, at least.* There's no penalty for asking for a discount. The flip side is *if there's anything in this world you want, and you don't have it, it's because you haven't asked for it, or let the world know you want it.*"

"I'm sorry, Kevin, but I disagree about everything being negotiable," Mac said. "What about when you're dealing with banks?"

Danielle jumped into the conversation. "A few words, please," she said, and without pausing, carried on. "Banks, our banks, are non-business businesses. Because they work with other people's money and are subject to public and regulatory scrutiny, they don't take risks. Because they're virtual monopolies they don't have to compete aggressively for our business, so they tend neither to understand, nor to learn how to do business with their clients. Because of the limited choices we have, we're forced to do business their way. The best way to find out what that means is to cultivate, at the least, a civil working relationship with a few tellers, and access to managers at as high a level of management as your value to the bank warrants."

"Go as high as you must to get what you need. And negotiate all the way. Try, anyway," Kevin said. "Granted, I had more clout than you do now, since about the time we had 10 debt-free stores spread around the country. As a buying group, they offered me a good foundation from which to negotiate deals with manufacturers. Well, they also made it easier for me to negotiate, from Toronto, a better deal on the costs of banking services than each store manager could get doing it locally."

"Wherever possible when you're negotiating, do it with the highest-positioned person you can find in a company or bank," Danielle said. "Because there's nothing so frustrating, or time wasting, as to negotiate a deal with someone, then have him or her say a higher-up has to approve the deal."

"So ask at the front end if the person you're dealing with is authorized to decide and sign for the company," Kevin said. "If the answer is no, don't waste time haggling, get an appointment with the decision maker. If that isn't possible...well, I'm hard line on this, walk out. My experience of not walking is the deal ends up costing more than it should, which cuts my margin and satisfaction, or is made so worthless I have to walk anyway, but have also wasted time in the process."

"Never fall for the 'It's policy.' line, either," Danielle added. "People often hide behind it. So, ask to see a policy in writing before you believe it exists. And if you are shown a policy, ask where it refers to you specifically. Just keep pressing for what you need."

. . . .

1990: *John Tan's Notes*

Great! I have a crush on my mentor's wife. No wonder he was able to do what he did with A Chip Off The Old Block having a partner like her. I mean they like each other, even love each other, and they're partners in what they do.

They have a division of labor that works, Danielle said, and she expects that as people start running more service businesses from home, there will be an increase in businesses run by husband and wife, or equivalent intimate partnerships. That arrangement will create its own kind of stresses, because the couple will be so much in contact under demanding and stressful conditions.

"Just keep in mind, that if partners are in an intimate relationship that's rocky, the business could be too. On the other hand, a strong relationship can make an excellent foundation for a business partnership," Danielle said. "The variables are many. What I came to appreciate the most is that for all his energy and creativity, Kevin is easier to work with than anyone else I've worked with. The personal intimacy makes for a deeper understanding of each other when we're working, and he has grown into a fine businessman."

"You mean he wasn't always like this?" I asked.

"No...in fact..." Danielle stared at me for a moment. "He was more like you when he started, ready to make a living at what he loved doing, selling a product he believed in. A bit naive about business. Brash..."

I think I blushed, and she smiled broadly at me, and winked.

"Until you find Ms. Right, John, I think you would do well to join a breakfast club, or some service organization that has regular business lunches, where you can network," Danielle suggested.

Kevin looked mystified. He had missed our little byplay. He shrugged and moved the talk back to spouses as partners.

"Yeah, but you walk a delicate balancing act, working with your spouse," he said. "Keeping the romance in the relationship, and out of the office, without damaging any of the value of the business or personal relationship with your spouse-business partner takes some sophisticated separation of ideas."

"Spouse-business partner? Is that what I am?" Danielle asked with a mugged and exaggerated expression of disappointment and a loud sigh.

Kevin shrugged. "Well, I'm searching for language that explains it," he said. "We started A Chip because you knew I was going crazy in my job. We had a buffer with your salary. When we got so big we needed someone to manage employee development and training, you were the logical choice, and, by then, you wanted to leave teaching."

"And the whole time we worked together, I never felt that your treatment of me was influenced by my being your wife. We acted sensibly," she said with a nod.

"Well, so much for language..."

"Hold on, though, there's another level of partnership we have to address, and that's the people you recruit to work for you, to whom you aren't related," Danielle said. "Kevin?"

He nodded. "You see, once A Chip started needing employees, I realized almost immediately that they were partners in our success, whether they had money at risk or not," Kevin said. "If they didn't believe and act according to the principles and values A Chip represented, and didn't give the high level of cheerful service that made our name, we were lost. That all had to be balanced with my belief that the only time you need a partner is when it's the only way you can recruit the talent you need to complement your own."

"You just lost me," I said.

"Well, I think partners should complement each other's skills, should make a whole greater than the two parts. Otherwise you have two underemployed people," Kevin said. "But I'll hire talent before I'll take on a partner. The only time I would go against that policy is when the price of getting the talent is a piece of the action. I'll retain control, but the financial arrangements take on a new dimension."

"I got it now," I said.

"So we had to come up with a way of ensuring our people knew we appreciated their work, while getting quality staff, and getting back from the staff the high degree of loyalty we gave them," Danielle said.

"We came up with the idea of incorporating each store as a separate entity, with The Old Block Ltd.—which Danielle and I, my brother, and my father owned—holding 95 per cent of the company," Kevin said. "The start-up manager had to buy a five per cent interest, which we would finance, and any employee could, after a year of working at any store, buy shares in the store, though we would never hold less than 60 per cent equity in each store."

"It worked for us," Danielle said. "But only because we treated everyone like a partner, from the day he or she started work with us."

"And what does 'treat everyone like a partner' mean?" I asked.

"Well, our people never thought of Kevin as a boss telling them what to do," Danielle said. "He was more like a coach, helping everyone pull the best performance out of themselves."

"Sounds pretty idealistic," I said.

"So who said you can't run a successful business and be decent about it?" Danielle demanded. "You know, we once had a woman apply for a job with us in Edmonton. She had been a top seller for a wholesale operation, but had been sexually harassed on the job, then was fired when she complained. She got a settlement, but couldn't get a job. I found out why when I called for references, and was led to believe, but not told outright, that she was a terrible employee, rotten person, and all around curse on humanity."

Kevin chuckled. "Oh, right, you'll all like this story," he said.

Danielle continued. "I had to be in Edmonton supervising a weekend staff development seminar on effective writing skills, and well...uh, contrived—"

"She went to see the manager who had been cited in the complaint, posing as a potential buyer," Kevin said with a smile.

"I would make a lousy spy," Danielle admitted. "But I carried it off, and came away from the meeting convinced that if that sexist bozo pinhead—"

"And Danielle is not a vocal or militant feminist, folks," Kevin announced.

"—thought that woman was the witch he described, and a terrible risk as an employee, we should hire her," Danielle said. "She almost worked herself to death in her first six months to enrich us all. We had to get her to slow down a bit and not burn out."

"She was running the Edmonton store, the third most profitable store in the chain, when we sold out," Kevin concluded.

"If you want a purely material measure of the success of our management design and ownership structures, John, consider that seven men and four women who started with A Chip in 1982 and 1983 had achieved their short-term personal investment goals—$100,000 in cash and securities, exclusive of houses and RRSPs—by the time we sold out," Danielle said.

"We didn't make life easy on anyone, not by any measure," Kevin said. "We set rigorous, but realistic goals and standards for ourselves and everyone else, and printed them, and detailed what company management would give in return. Everyone who came to work for us had to read those goals and standards, what we required of them, and our return obligations, and sign them. And we all acted every day as the partners we became."

"It wasn't all roses and chocolate in performance, though," Danielle said. "We provided a positive, growth enhancing work environment that required self discipline of the participants, and some of them just couldn't handle it."

"Some!?" Kevin said in astonishment. "Many! The degree of enmeshment in traditional, rigid employer-employee relations some of them displayed made them wholly inflexible and unable to adjust to our working environment. Our staff churn factors in the early days were unacceptably high," he said with disgust. "That's one of the key reasons we ran the continual training and education programs. If we couldn't find people with the attitudes we needed to succeed, we would do our best to help them liberate themselves."

"You know, there's an even better measure of the success of your management system than the people who met their retirement investment goals by '90," I said.

"Oh, what?" Danielle asked.

"A Chip Off The Old Block itself," I replied.

CHAPTER ELEVEN

Going to Market

1995, The Conference: *Day Two, Morning*

"Good morning. Welcome to Day Two of our conference," Kieron said to the delegates. "We have no housekeeping matters to worry about, so we'll get on to the business at hand. This session, *'Selling, Marketing, Loyalty Management: Who's hyping Who?'*, promises to be an interesting one. Our moderator is Danielle Short, a founding partner of A Chip Off The Old Block, who left teaching in 1984 to establish and manage the company's employee assistance and training functions. In 1987, she also became director of marketing for The Old Block, the parent company. She is now vice-president of Big Chip Management, in partnership with Kevin Short."

When the applause died down, Danielle introduced the panelists sharing the stage with her, then launched into her opening remarks.

"The world of market researchers, pollsters and analysts is a carnival of characters. They range from those who affect the air of aging, defiant hippies amused by the 'straight world', who laugh all the way to the bank as they show the suits how to do business through the quiet effective ones, to the young go-getters who actually wear Armani suits, with white-on-white shirts, red power suspenders and have had neuro-linguistic training which allows them to connect with the client on that 'deeply personal level'.

"Whatever the face they present, marketers have become caricatures, stereotypes who have risen from the mythology the market consultants have created for themselves as brilliant number crunchers who can point to a product and say, 'Package it this way. Advertise it this way. Price it this way. And it will sell.'

"Marketers have set themselves up as a new priesthood of capitalism, but in the process, have so badly marketed what they actually do that the world thinks they are the pitchmen who get up in the TV Infomercials and tell you how they're going to change your life in the next 30 minutes."

....

1990: *A Lecture Hall*

"It's always important to be conscious of where we've been while we're on the road to where we're going, just in case we need to move back a few steps to get our bearings, or adjust course," Kevin said. "My father taught us the idea, but I learned it when I saw it in action. I was still a green young salesman, doing my time in Calgary, when I met Ray Kinnear..."

Ray, of an old breed of field geologists who actually walked the ground on which they discovered oil, divided his time between remote northern locations managing projects, and a high-rise office tower. When he wasn't doing either, he was working with another fellow to manage a working guest ranch they held in partnership, to which tourists, business people needing a change, and fantasists would come and pay for the privilege of doing ranch work.

Kevin and Ray were trying to close a deal on a computer system for Ray's company, but had been playing telephone tag for days. Finally, Ray had left Kevin a message to meet him at a crossroads south of the city, at a particular time on a particular day. Ray met him with a four-wheel-drive pick-up, and drove in to the ranch on a dirt road that would have been impassable to Kevin's car because a recent thaw and two days of rain had turned it into a bog.

As he drove, Ray kept looking over his shoulder. He didn't use the rear-view mirror; he just kept looking over his shoulder. Mystified, Kevin asked him why he was doing this. "Are you worried about thought police in the bush?" he joked.

Ray shook his head. "It's a habit I picked up flying my own plane in the bush in northern Canada. It's always good to have a sight picture of what the way back looks like, just in case you have an emergency and have to turn around."

Kevin turned and looked back, and immediately saw what Ray was talking about.

"So, before we discuss marketing, and just what it is and how it will help you in business, we're going to look at where it came from, and that's the world of selling," Kevin said. "And to start, I'll pose the question: What is salesmanship? Anyone?"

"It's the ability to sell," Anne Porter called out.

"Good," Kevin said. "Anything else?"

"Isn't that enough? John Tan demanded.

"Try: '*It's the ability to discern what will make a person want to buy your product from among competing products, and from all the other things he or she feels the need to buy, and to act on that understanding.*'" Kevin said. "But let's put selling in a context. Salesmanship has its historical basis in the days when companies were focused on moving product. When the main concern was how to most efficiently and effectively move product from the manufacturer to the customer through a distribution channel..."

. . . .

1990: *John's Notes*

So, Kevin used market researchers and consultants when he was running A Chip. But Mindworks? The big sharks in the game. I called him on that, because all the hype about A Chip, and him, when he was the darling of the business media, was that he was a great natural merchant, a vendor with marketing smarts.

"The people at Mindworks were only my advisors and research consultants," Kevin said. "I always make my own decisions, and they're best made when we follow our instincts. Our instincts, however, work best when they're informed, but I couldn't be in 12 places at once, so I hired them to gather information." He started putting another sheet on the overhead machine, then he turned to me and said, "John, if I thought a witch doctor throwing bones would give me information I needed to make a critical decision, I'd talk with him. I just wouldn't let him nor ask him to make my decision for me." Then he went on.

Salesmanship was the tool used to maximize sales and profits. The most vivid image to illustrate the salesman is what some people call the 'Herb Tarlek' approach of the fast-talking, high-pressure salesman who would sell people things they didn't really feel they needed. There was a heavy emphasis on high-pressure tactics, on closing the sale. Follow-up customer satisfaction was never seen as a big element of the transaction, because there were always so many other people to sell to.

"So, *salesmanship is a transaction involving something that has been made and is put on offer to potential clients, who are urged to buy it,*" Kevin said. "We can even talk about the mass market/mass industry/consumerist era beginning its rise around 1945, to what I believe was its peak in 1975. You see, during World War Two, we had huge increases in manufacturing capability." He gestured with his hands, sculpting the world he was talking about in the air. "Then, after the war, the demand for products was huge. There was the pent-up demand from the Depression, when people had no money to spend on anything but necessities, and the war years, when people earned large amounts of disposable income, but, because of rationing, could only spend some of it on necessities, which left them holding cash or war bonds. The war was also when we developed tremendous amounts of factory and production capability. So, after the war, this wild buying spree began…"

At that point, selling was a function of how quickly manufacturers could match what people wanted (of which they wanted a lot), to what they could supply. Salesmanship almost took the form of simple order taking. A salesman didn't really have to do much selling, because people wanted whatever he was selling.

So manufacturers said, 'This is great. Let's build more capacity.' and people said, 'Let's keep buying things.' A lot of order taking went on, and the salesman—in the store, door-to-door, the travelling salesman, the industrial salesman—had his heyday from about 1945 to 1970.

"Now add in the development of consumerism, which occurs when manufacturers have met the pent-up demand," Kevin said. "Your market is sated, but you have to keep your factory busy if you're to remain prosperous and wealthy. We also get the development of the marketing function, during what I call the consumerist age, both of which were spurred by the rapid increase of consumer credit easily available to large portions of the population…"

Manufacturers faced a new challenge. Where before they were concerned with getting product to a receptive public, now they had to get the public to choose their product from among a range of directly and indirectly competing product options.

"And we have the rise of marketing, which is really about perception," Kevin said. "For example, my product is better than that product. Or more desirable. Or will cause a higher degree of envy/anxiety among your neighbors. *Marketing,*" Kevin said in that tone of voice I've come to recognize means WRITE THIS DOWN, "*is not about my reality as a manufacturer. It is about the reality of consumers and the words and images that move them. How effectively an organization uses those determines how successful it will be in the marketplace.*"

I said: "Marketing is simply satisfying customer needs, right?"

"Almost," Kevin nodded. "It's discerning client needs, and meeting them, while meeting organizational goals, which, we hope, are about making money by selling a particular product. The key difference is, though, a product seller will talk about products and talk about maximizing sales and revenue in an efficient way while keeping the cost base at a minimum level. A *marketer* will say, '*What I want to do is satisfy customers. What I am most interested in is designing products and services that meet customers' needs, so I can get better margins, retain loyalty, and meet my organization's mission, to make profits.*"

"I have an even better summary," Brenda said. "Selling is moving product, while marketing is defining and satisfying customer need."

"Exactly," Kevin said. "Moving items is the product orientation; meeting needs is the marketing orientation. When I'm sitting and talking to you as product seller, what I'm thinking is, 'How do I get Brenda to buy this?', and if I were a marketer I'd be thinking 'Does Brenda even want this?', and maybe I should be going back and finding some other product for Brenda and all the other Brendas who want or need that product."

So, just to summarize it another way: a product seller looks through his eyes; a marketer looks through the customer's eyes. The key is a concept Kevin calls positioning. The marketer positions the product as a solution to a consumer's problem, meeting the need. That works if you're dealing in either goods or services. The idea is to become identified in the consumers'/clients' minds as solutions to problems.

Omigod! that's what that line means, the one that goes, *You get what you want out of life by helping other people get what they want out of life.*

I see! I see! *Marketing is a way of thinking,* and it goes: as much as I want to achieve my own goals, the only way I'm going to achieve my goals is by forming relationships with customers and seeing the world through their eyes, seeing what they value, and helping them acquire what bolsters that sense of value and values. It means: *Focus on the person and the need, not the product.*

This marketing orientation means we can target particular market segments. If we know 18- to 24-year-old males identify beer, sex, rock and roll and good times, and I'm a brewer trying to penetrate that market, then I have to skew the advertising so it gets across the messages youth=beer=sex=rock 'n' roll.

"Kevin, if I look at my proposed business through mainland Chinese eyes, my biggest challenge in selling myself as an industrial agent in China, is my youth," I said.

"Right! So your first job is to position that as a strength," Kevin said. "Help the Chinese understand that our culture makes the inexcusable error of venerating the energy of youth over the wisdom of age, but you, brought up in a traditional Chinese household, even in North America, venerate age. So you can solve the basic communications problems between brash North Americans and China's elders because of your bi-cultural experience. Do that, and you'll have sold your services, in a cultural context, without having to sell the services themselves."

"It might work," I said. "I'll talk with my cousin about this."

"Another thing you have to watch for is that market researchers and consultants run the gamut of brilliant to monkeys filling blanks," Kevin said. "And they make mistakes."

"Like the new Coke/Classic Coke fiasco?" Susan asked.

"Now you see, Coke is a marketing company, first and foremost, yet it changed the Coke recipe in reaction to the marketing perception that younger people drank Pepsi, because it was sweeter, and older people would be switching to Pepsi, because they identified with the youth idea," Kevin said. "So out with the old. In with the new. And a loyal clientele goes nuts."

"So, was it all just a set up to reposition Coke Classic, and grab off new market from Pepsi?" Susan asked.

Kevin shrugged. "I'm not privy to decisions made at Coke's Atlanta headquarters, and nobody has ever admitted to anything. We can only speculate."

"I have one for you," said Marcella Dion, a slight, older woman who had moved to Toronto from Montreal for the duration of the program. "A food company that had made a ground beef processed food to put on buns, with an English name like Sloppy Joe, wanted to move the product into the Quebec market, but had to make a French name for the product. It was a terrible mistake, because the words they chose are a direct translation, but, in French, the phrase is a vulgar way of describing a woman with, um—" She rolled her hands in front of her, as she struggled for the right words. "—big breasts."

"My sister-in-law is from Panama," Anne Porter said. "And she has this *Gringo* thing, thinks Americans are rude and ignorant people for the way they treat anyone who isn't American. She says everyone got a big laugh when they tried selling a car called Nova in Latin America. It was perfect for the marketplace, sturdy, reliable, low-cost, high gas-mileage engine, except Nova in Spanish means 'does not go'. And no one wanted a car that advertised it wouldn't go in its very own name."

It took a while for everyone to settle down after that story. Kevin kept chuckling between sentences as he tried to get the session back on track.

"Now we have to distinguish between market researchers and marketers," Kevin said, as he fought the urge to keep laughing. "The researchers do the figuring out. Marketers do the selling. Good, effective salespeople are natural marketers, but marketers don't necessarily know how to sell."

He looked at us with a crooked grin, then asked: "What's the definition of a consultant?"

"An expert," Susan called out.

"Try, someone who knows 77 ways to make love, but can't get a date."

The answer was so unexpected, we were all stunned a moment, then were suddenly roaring with laughter again.

"Mind you, you could say the same thing about an expert," Kevin chuckled. "About '84, the marketing philosophy hit, and the language of careers ads changed from 'Salesperson wanted' to 'Marketer wanted' and everyone began hiring commerce grads and MBAs, then couldn't understand why their sales slumped and even took years to recover. You remember the woman Danielle told you about, the salesperson who ended up running our Edmonton store?"

"The sexual harassment case," Brenda said.

"That's right," Kevin said.

Her name was Anna, and her observation was: "What employers don't understand, is that a good salesperson with even only five years of experience knows what marketing is without going to school for it." Anna had mastered the idea of service, which is simply to meet a client's needs promptly, efficiently, and cheerfully enough that the client feels valued. "The employers saw the degrees as a substitute for experience, and expected they would be effective from Day One. But no one, even a natural salesperson, knows all the techniques of selling right away. People might have the inclination, even a talent for selling, but it takes time to develop the selling skill."

So, as she saw it, whether it was marketer or seller, the person presenting the products for sale and taking the orders—in retail, wholesale, or the service business—is working with a client, developing a relationship, finding out what the client needs, and presenting the product to solve a problem. Closing the sale means going the next step and saying something like, 'And that will be how many dozen? What colors? To be delivered when?' Even then, the sale isn't complete until the goods have been delivered to the satisfaction of the client, and the seller is in there preparing the client for the next sale.

"One of the secrets of A Chip's success, and it isn't that much of a secret," said Kevin, "is that we had return clientele. Buying paper, or a ribbon, or a printer, or a computer, was like a visit to an old friend. If you want it in the words of my 'expert' contact at Mindworks—"

He put up an overhead, which read:

> In the competitive marketplace we have today, the ones establishing long-term and consistent relationships with their customers are the ones that are doing better. The other people are basically spending a lot of money strictly on advertising and price cutting, and what they're doing is trading customers all the time. Trading customers and getting new customers is probably the most expensive way to do business. So, the big winners today are the ones that are marketing oriented and see their business as customer satisfaction and building long-term relationships.

. . . .

1995: *The Conference*

"Since the economic turbulence we've been experiencing hit us hard in 1989, there have been profound shifts in the marketplace," Danielle said. "This next slide will show you the value-set profiles of Canadian consumers today." She nodded to a young man at an overhead projector.

A table filled the screen. It read:

TODAY'S CONSUMER

TRADITIONAL VALUES	STATUS-SEEKING & SOCIAL-RECOGNITION VALUES
Belief in tradition, security, church and state, financial concern for the future, saving on principle, utilitarian consumerism, confidence in business. Conformist, but with shadings of rugged individualism.	Belief in ostentatious consumption, the joy of consumption, concern for appearances, confidence in advertising and business. Marked by attitude: I am what I buy, and who you think I am. Relatively conformist, but really cares what other people think.
Popular culture icons: Father Knows Best; The Walton Family	Popular culture icons: Alex P. Keaton character in Family Ties; the character of Gordon Gekko in Wall Street—Mr. 'Greed is good!'
Strong in WASP English Canada	Strong in Quebec
ME GENERATION VALUES	EXPERIENCE-SEEKING & NEW MENTAL FRONTIERS VALUES
Liberal, freedom-focused beliefs. Control of one's own destiny, rejection of order and authority, scepticism towards business, spontaneity, adaptability to the complexity of life, anything that stresses freedom. Strong sense of equality. Focus on values that say equality is important, because it allows individual freedom.	Belief in novelty, essentialism, the world is a potpourri of exciting experiences, the importance of feeling life to the maximum. Life is a slalom course, and that which is not fun is to be navigated around, and that which is fun is to be navigated to. The world is a global village, and global experience can be had locally by tapping into the technological highways of the world—CNN, MTV, computer networks.
Popular culture icons for this value set include Murphy Brown, Alan Alda as Hawkeye Pearce in MASH.	A highly visual, sensual value set that has as popular culture icons Super Dave Osborne, and Nintendo.

"These are the values held by the people you want to sell goods or services to," Danielle said. "What you provide must speak to, meet, enhance, or otherwise validate some or all of those value sets. But you must be prepared for the economic equivalent of guerrilla warfare. The consumer has declared war on sellers."

Danielle waited for the hum of conversation that erupted at her statement to die down.

"Traditional loyalties to brand names and store names are eroding—not breaking, just eroding. As they erode, the market-oriented seller's concern is still to maintain customer loyalty...and loyalty management is the new marketing technique," she said. "But, in the retail business particularly, cost-cutting isn't the only effective answer any more." She held up a handful of plastic cards and waved them. "Rather, retailers are working marketing as a loyalty management game with points bonus programs like Air Miles, Club Z points, Bay Bucks, Sears Club, American Express, etc. They're all offering incentives to buy exclusively in their stores, with their credit cards, or from groups of retailers who honor the car or program. They are recruiting long-term consumer loyalty to the card or supplier group by providing the incentive of bonus rewards."

"But I'm not in retailing," someone called from the audience. "I rent brain time."

"Service suppliers have it tougher, no question about it," Danielle agreed. "What kind of incentive program can you offer except quality and price breaks? But cutting your fees makes you vulnerable to going broke. You still, however, have to establish client loyalty, so you get return work, by delivering high-quality service, and keep driving home the message, whenever you bid on a project, that the cheapest bid on a project doesn't necessarily offer the best solution to the problem. Mac?"

"The security business sells peace of mind, which could involve anything from silent alarms to full-time bodyguards," Mac said. "All of that is hard to position, even though personal safety is among the top three concerns voiced by Canadians."

Danielle nodded to the overhead operator and the new slide that came up on the screen read:

THE SERVICE MARKETING CHALLENGE

1. Do prospective clients even see the problem as a problem? (So there's an educational element to our positioning— we sometimes have to show clients there *is* a problem.)

2. We have to show them the problem has a cost—eroded sense of well being, lost earnings, depressed earnings.

3. We have to show them we are the best to do the job.

Mac pointed to the screen, and said: "These have always been, and always will be, the challenges we face as service marketers."

"Well, many of the independents who are leaders in their fields consider some sort of public speaking or teaching as important elements in their business, as much because they give something to their communities, as to position themselves as leaders in providing their particular goods or services," Danielle said. "Laura Gunderson, the psychologist who was one of the first consultants to A Chip Off The Old Block, isn't comfortable with the 'let's do lunch' schmooze thing, but she loves giving seminars, and radio interviews, which have helped her develop a profile as an expert. So people know who she is because they've heard her speak, or they've read articles by or about her." Danielle looked around the room, and asked, "Remember the fireworks yesterday?"

The room was filled with murmuring as people excitedly recalled the small light show of the evening before.

"The fellow who set that up is Daniel Best, The Pyro Guy," Danielle said. "He takes a few days a few times each year to speak in industry workshops and seminars about special effects and pyrotechnics. He even gets to show off some of his stuff..."

There's a bonus in all this for Daniel. He's gregarious, an important quality in business, and he likes his work and business. Next to designing, creating, and executing special effects and pyro shows, he loves talking about them, and showing off some of the toys and principles that govern the business. He also gets honoraria and his expenses paid for these performances.

Besides the occasional workshop and seminar, Daniel takes a few days a year to teach an introduction to special effects and pyrotechnics to theatre and film arts students here, at Oswego College. Again, in this instance, he gets to show off his stuff, talk about what he does, and take a break from his usual way of doing business. A smart fellow, he thinks it would be nice if he connects with potential clients, but he doesn't make that the reason he takes on the teaching—it would take the fun out of it, make it seem like work, and destroy his enthusiasm.

Daniel finds that the less he is concerned with making the teaching a business development opportunity, the more the teaching leads to business. "Think of it," he said to Kevin. "These people might be in business for 20 or 30 years, and I'm the guy they think of first to buy effects and pyrotechnics and supplies from, because I'm the guy who introduced the subject to them. They'll come back because I give them good prices, high quality product, and excellent service."

Danielle nodded as Kevin concluded his story. "The key is to look at the consumer culture we're in now and see where you fit and how to position yourself to make money from providing products and services to people in the '90s, a decade that's fundamentally different from the '80s," she said. "In the '80s, we operated in a market characterized by social symbolism, and people bought products and services because other people liked and valued them. In the '90s, we're dealing in *personal symbolism.* So, more and more, people are buying products and services because *they like them themselves.* That's led to the erosion of the impact of big brand names, because social symbolism was why people bought them..."

The new consumer as guerrilla is a person who comes into a store, restaurant, service business, whatever, with the basic attitude: First of all, I'm not sure I want to be here at all. Second, I want to keep my options open. Third, I'm smarter and better informed than the average person who's selling to me, and a better negotiator. This has resulted in something researchers are now calling 'Reach For The Top'.

Consumers today don't want to deal with salespeople; they want to deal with the people who own the businesses. It's the same reason why, to a certain degree, entrepreneurship is growing, because more people want to deal with the president; they don't want to deal with the staff. Ask retailers today how they spend most of their time, and they'll tell you more of it than before is spent with customers.

"And customers want to deal, folks, more than ever," Danielle said. "And a big part of it has to do with learning that what we all thought were rules, and were told were rules, are just practices... flexible practices. We had a customer in Winnipeg, Bob Gullison. Talk about loyalty. He bought his first computer from Kevin in 1983, through one of those writers' associations deals. This fellow was delighted when we opened a store in Winnipeg, and bought all his supplies from us, and every one of the three computer upgrades he bought from then to 1989. Anyway, he told us something he learned..."

Bob was pricing vacuum cleaners, and expressed his frustration about the difficulty of deciding where to buy the model he had targeted, because prices varied so drastically from outlet to outlet. A salesman shrugged and said he would match the best price. Now this was at The Grange, a department store, where any of us who grew up in Canada in the '50s and '60s and '70s learned that to challenge the posted price was tantamount to breaking wind in the presence of the Queen.

"We, ah, have some leeway in the large appliances section," the salesman admitted.

The earth moved for Bob, but he didn't buy the vacuum cleaner there. A few months later, though, he was back in the same store, same floor, looking for a new phone answering machine. It happened that he had just begun experimenting with writing incidental music to accompany some writing projects he was working on, and was planning to buy a piano, so he could improve his theory skills and formal training. He noticed around Christmas The Grange had brought in a line of up-market electronic pianos with three-quarter-sized keyboards. They were priced at $1,499.

In the New Year, he was back at the store, and the pianos were marked down to $999. For about a week, he thought about the piano, remembered what the salesman had said, and decided to go in the next day and offer $750 for one of the pianos. When Bob arrived, a price plaque on the display model announced 50 per cent off. He searched out the salesman he had spoken to before and asked, "Fifty per cent off retail or the last ticket price?"

"The last ticket price," the salesman said.

"Sold at $499.50," Bob said.

"The key issue here is *the customer wants to deal*, because the concepts of value for our money, what money means to us, and what we do to get it have changed or broadened somewhat," Danielle said. "Whatever the reason for negotiating—the need to wheel and deal, the need to make money go further, personal values that tell us asking prices are too high, or that a transaction loses meaning if there isn't some negotiation built into it—it's the new selling environment. *We earn customer loyalty by negotiating for it and performing according to what we negotiated.*"

CHAPTER TWELVE

Doing Business

1990: *The College Coffee Bar*

"...all I'm saying is that probably the toughest act most businesspeople have to perform is committing words to paper," Danielle said. "That's why I sent Kevin back to school."

"Get out of here!" John Tan said. "You sent the boss back to school?"

"With instructions to pass, or do it again," Danielle nodded. "He was trained as an engineer, and then he did his MBA. Where would he have had the chance to study and practise effective language skills?"

"What kind of hold do you have on that guy?" Susan asked.

"The best kind," Danielle laughed. "I want to see him grow into the finest person he can become."

"But to send him back to school..." John muttered.

"It's leadership by example, John," Mac interjected. "You can't expect your people to trust you, be loyal to you, and perform to your standards if you don't offer them the honesty of adhering to the standards yourself. And not by lip service, but by action."

"What do you think you're doing, John?" Danielle asked. She then asked all of Kevin's proteges, "What do you think lifelong learning is?"

"But he's made his mark, and his fortune," Brenda said.

"He could even have made his fortune in marks, if he'd had the yen," John grinned.

Everyone groaned.

"I won't miss your awful puns when we're done this program," Mac said. "I know what you mean, Danielle. We were studying all the time in the military. Basic training taught us the basic skills— marching, shooting, field hygiene, reading maps, that sort of thing. Then we specialized in some technical trade, management or operational specialty, and we were constantly studying because a good part of the decision on promotions was based on examination results. We even had formal writing courses."

"Really, Mac, why?" Danielle asked.

"Well, we had to learn to write precise, concise, clear communiques, because the chaos of battle is a bad time to be telling someone you don't understand the orders you've been given," Mac said.

"We don't have to contend with battle in business, but we do have to think and write clearly," Danielle said. "And the two are opposite sides of the same coin. In business we need clearly written, effective communications materials that serve three purposes: present our business, what it does, and what it stands for, to our public; form the record of our business, and its performance; and quickly and easily transmit information to our stakeholders—ourselves, employees, partners, sub-contractors, investors, for example."

"But you would think he'd have learned that stuff in school," Brenda said. "He's articulate."

"Yes, he is. That's a product of his disciplines of thought and habit, combined with the language skills he learned," Danielle said. "But the school system doesn't effectively teach language skills as life skills."

"So why did you send him back to school?" John asked.

"Well, actually, I asked that writer in Winnipeg what to do, and he told me about another writer he knew in Calgary—a real maniac about effective communications—who taught an effective writing program in night school. So, when we opened the second Calgary store, Kevin did the opening himself, and took the course."

"I think it's wonderful, the way you used the business to make so much happen in your lives," Brenda said.

"What other reason is there to be in business?" Danielle asked.

"Money!" John said.

"Now that's interesting, John, because the only people I know whose only business interest is money are the people with jobs," Danielle said. "I don't know if we could have built A Chip the way we did if we had only been in it for the money, though it's an important motivator. Why, it wasn't until Store Three was open that Kevin suggested we just take it as far as it would go, and we formalized the grand plan of building a national chain of stores."

"That still amazes me," John said.

"How do you think it made us feel?" Danielle laughed. "Anyway, it gave me the opportunity to experiment with making the business a learning environment. No one was required ever to take a course, but everyone could take the courses we set up for personal financial management, self esteem, language skills, sales skills, or we would pay three-quarters of the cost of out-of-house courses."

"And what happened?"

"Better to ask what we accomplished," Danielle said. "But I'll save you the effort. We found our earnings per square foot in each store increased and stayed better with each course our people took, or each program I set up for the staff. When a management consultant came in to analyze why, our people said they felt like part of a family, where their interests were as important to management as management's. They also had a vested interest in the success of the business, so they worked harder, but never felt exploited."

Kevin came rushing to the table. "Hi. Sorry I'm late. The faculty meeting went long," he said as he took a seat.

"Who won?" John asked.

"Won?" Kevin asked back.

"You always talk about the meetings as if they were combat," Mac explained.

Kevin sat back and thought a moment. "You're right. You guys won."

"How's that?" Brenda asked.

"I argued that we've covered everything possible that could be done in class," Kevin said. "You should be concentrating on your labs, and writing your business plans, and..."

"I don't like the sound of that 'and...'," Brenda said. "What have you done, Kevin?"

"Well, everyone gets to do a two-week internship in some retail stores in Toronto, Ottawa, and London."

"More expense," Brenda groaned.

"Not at all," Kevin smiled. "You get stipends and full commissions on anything you sell. And meals and accommodations are being provided by the Amity Hotels Group. That's why we picked Ottawa and London."

"How did you arrange all this?" Susan wondered.

"Ask Danielle," Kevin said. "She set it up."

"How?" Brenda demanded.

"I just showed everyone how it was in their best interests to help," Danielle said. "Of course, it helps that they're also all part of the Elmag holdings…"

....

1995: *The Conference*

"Thank you for participating in this conference," Kieron said. "I hope that when you return to your homes, your businesses, or your government offices, you think positively and hopefully about the future."

There was applause.

"We are witnessing ongoing rapid change in our society and the world that has people confused, concerned about making it through each day, and worried about the future. You are the vanguard of change. I'm glad, and proud, that Oswego College, my brother Kevin, my sister-in-law Danielle, and I have had a chance to help people make sense of change, and show how to make change our partner, not our enemy."

As he spoke, the screen descended from the ceiling, and the lights began to dim.

"Before Kevin and Danielle come to say their final words to you, we would like to show you a film prepared specifically for this part of the program."

The lights came down on his last words, and images flickered on the screen. *Money,* from Pink Floyd's *Dark Side of The Moon* album came from the public address system, and was the soundtrack to a montage of quick cuts under the title, *Five Years and Counting*. The images established the locations in the story by taking quick shots of distinctive skylines or other features.

The first cuts were shot through greenery, over the heads of diners, through windows onto a waterway… It was a shot from Vancouver's Granville Island, overlooking False Creek. Then it cut to a downtown street and a shot of the distinctive Calgary Tower. The next shot was a pan of the theatres on Toronto's King Street, and a rooftop cutaway to the Skydome.

The dome segued back to Vancouver, to a restaurant overlooking False Creek, and Brenda Bashford appeared on screen, to introduce the place as hers, the Garden of Eatin'. She described the restaurant, its operations and clientele. Then she paused to look out a window, and the camera followed her gaze to a man on the quay, looking across the water. The camera zoomed in on the figure. It was John Tan.

"There's north. There's east," he said jabbing a forefinger at the compass points. Then he pointed to the west. "Hong Kong, my cousin, the other half of my business are there. To the elders of China, my cousin and I are just young pups, with much to learn. They watch us carefully, but they've learned I'm useful as a bridge between their cultural perspectives on age and wisdom, and North America's cult of youth."

As he talked, John walked along the quay, and came to a display of contemporary Native art, and a big sign reading Sweetgrass Native Art Corp. The camera came in tight on the logo, then pulled back, and in the full shot, the logo was now on a door, which opened, and Susan Manyfingers came through.

She then walked the viewers through the building that housed Sweetgrass Native Art Corp., a decommissioned school in an older Calgary neighborhood that had been transformed into a native art and cultural centre. In a music room, a six-piece band accompanied singers and dancers as they rehearsed a native rock opera called *Brother Eagle*. Classrooms were being used as studios by artists working in paints, pottery and silver, and the old auditorium was an art gallery alive with brilliantly colored native art.

"In the two years the place has been operating, we have shipped to galleries and clients in Asia and Europe more than 2,000 pieces of art," Susan said. "They were all pre-sold from catalogues created with the help of the artists in our print and design studio." She opened her arms in an expansive gesture. "All this came about because I had a vision. The money was available, but I had to be able to do my business my way, and I had to know how the world wanted me to do business. Well, I learned, and here we are."

She led the camera to the front door, and introduced the building security manager, who wore a uniform with a shoulder flash reading, Veterans Security. He led the camera through the big glass doors into a big office, where Mac sat behind a desk, talking on the phone. Behind him, the Skydome loomed large in his window.

Mac hung up, rose and welcomed the viewers, then led the camera out of his office down the hall to the Veterans command centre. A large map of Canada was inscribed on a plexiglass wall. Red lights showed the Veterans regional offices in Vancouver, Calgary, Toronto, Montreal and Halifax. A little forest, hundreds of green lights, glowed across the country, showing where Veterans Security people were operating in teams, or singly on everything from bodyguard services for visiting VIPs, to warehouse vigils.

The film ended on the steps of Oswego College, just below the big sign that read, *The Oswego College Entrepreneurship Incubator. We Hatch Success.*

The image held for an extended closing; then, as it flickered out, the lights came up and Danielle and Kevin came on stage, hand-in hand, and went to the microphone as the audience applauded the film.

"Hello, everyone," Danielle began. "We're here so Kevin can have the last word—"

"He always gets the last word!" John Tan called from where he sat with Mac and Brenda.

"No, he doesn't. I do," Danielle laughed, and the audience laughed with her. "Except today. Even I haven't heard what he has prepared for you, so I'll leave the stage to him." She kissed him on the cheek, and left the stage.

Kevin waited until Danielle was seated, before he began. "When we ran the pilot program five years ago, which seems an eternity, we had one goal only: to show you, as much as possible, what you would face when you got out there, into that mythical place we call the real world, to do business.

"It would be unfair of me to stand here and tell you what a great job we're doing, though I only have to look at you, read the list of successes you've made, to know we're all succeeding with this program. However, among the letters many of you have written me since you were in the program was one that came to me just before I went to Russia for the college. I've carried it around with me since.

"The letter is from Ron Brooks, a thirtysomething fellow who was part of the second-year group. Even though I always argued that with the right preparation you could make a living at anything, my own faith was tested when he began developing the plan for his business. This is what he says:

'Dear Kevin,

'It is now six years since I lost my job as a middle manager in a plastics company, four since I got into the Oswego program.

'Talk about a devastated life. First the job loss, then my wife divorced me. At least we didn't have any kids. For almost two years, I worked at getting another job in my field, but it just didn't work. My heart wasn't in it. I mean I had been a good kid, did what my parents directed, went to university, married my high school sweetheart, got a good job like everyone wanted me to, and lived a nice, orderly life. But when I lost my job, my nice, tidy world turned inside out.

'I have to admit, I was dissatisfied with my job, and my life. Most of what I did, I did to please other people...family, wife, in-laws. You know the routine. Just about the only pleasure I got towards the end of my job and marriage was when I would come home from work and lock myself in the den and play the piano, and mess with song ideas for a couple of hours to unwind. I got more life and energy from 20 minutes at the keyboard than I got from a week at work.

'You remember what Laura Gunderson said, when she was a guest speaker at one of our sessions? "Any shock that causes one's sense of self to be turned upside down has the effect of making a person rethink his or her life." She has my vote on that.

'I remember how concerned even you were, when I said I wanted to perform professionally, and write music. It must have been that you're like most people. You listen to music, but really never registered, until I came along with my plans, that people write it, and make money—sometimes damned good money—at it. But you said that if we can commercialize an idea, we're in business. That's what I wanted to do with my musical abilities.

'Do you remember how amazed you were when I researched the business and found out just how much money a person could make writing and selling songs? Remember when I brought in the estimate that Paul McCartney was worth about $800 million, with most of his fortune built on money from song royalties?

'And then I showed you the list of other songwriters and what they earned. Now, I knew making it big is rare, and maybe I'm not one of the few birds that will soar to those heights, but I also knew I'd never find out if I didn't spread my wings, flap them around, and make a little noise. So, I continued my research and wrote my plan. By the way, just so you have something else to be boggled about, all the big name acts that toured in 1994 up to the end of that summer—the Eagles, Pink Floyd, the Rolling Stones and such—grossed more than $1.25 billion. Not bad for a half year's work.

'Anyway, I examined every way performers screwed up their careers, and I worked hard to avoid those mistakes. Remember what we went through with the college bureaucracy so I could take conservatory classes in preparation for taking my Grade Eight Practical and Grade Two Theory exams with the Royal Ontario Conservatory of Music, just so I could be qualified to teach music, as a backstop?

'Well, I haven't taught any music lessons, but, while doing the conservatory work, I brushed up certain of my skills enough that I'm in demand as an arranger. More importantly, though, all the time I've worked as a musician, I've followed your injunction to be businesslike in all my affairs, and, as you suggested in another lecture, every day I live a life I've defined for myself. It has been hard at times, mostly keeping myself up and positive, facing the fears—of failure, and success—being my best friend and moral compass to success with dignity. But, I remind myself, no one asked me to be a musician. It's a decision I'm glad I made.

'For a year, I played every place I could, to get used to audiences, to develop the entertainer in me, to try out my own songs. I played some pretty divey places, and some wonderful places. Then, as I became better at being an entertainer, I got booked into better places, playing a mix of cover tunes, old standards and my own songs.

'Here's something you said. It's from my notes of your farewell class to us:

'"When you are out there, no matter what business you go into, you'll meet saints and sinners, poets and pushers, prophets and pimps. You'll see the best of people and the worst of people. Why? Business is a product of society, so it reflects society. We have the good, the bad, the indifferent in society, and they all show up in business. It isn't anything personal. How they treat you is how they treat everyone."

'But you also told us we didn't have to settle for abusive treatment, that we have the right to say no to doing things we don't believe in, or feel unsafe or ashamed or embarrassed to do. Well, I said no a few times, and was kicked out of a couple of places. I stood and fell on the principle: *Do not become a co-venturer in your own exploitation.*

'Two bar managers even tried to blacklist me, one after I refused to kick back part of my fees to him, the other because he tried to stiff me for the rest of my fees. It was a risk. My agent was ready to let me hang, told me that was the way the business ran.

'I told him that was unacceptable, and I really didn't want to change the world, but I wasn't going to play that way. The musician's union stepped in and straightened out the mess, at my request, and I got a new agent, who put me into better gigs, away from the bar network those sleazoid managers were on. Like you kept saying, I have options. I have always had options. I just didn't know I had to give myself permission to exercise them. I also had to learn that if you do business with slime, on slime's level, you get slimed, and I've learned to listen for the signals that someone isn't exactly a straight shooter.

'"There will be days when you spell self employment as *UNEMPLOYMENT,* and wonder why you ever bothered taking this route," you said. "You'll wonder, those days after you've paid the taxman, the postman, the employees, the suppliers, the dues collector, and everyone else but yourself, if there isn't a better way. But keep at it, develop your business and yourself, and the day will come when you wonder that you ever doubted yourself.

'"That's how you grow your business—by growing yourself. Keep an open mind. Don't take anything personally. And if something is personal, lay it aside. Don't waste time beating yourself up and selling yourself short—there are enough people who will do that for you. And if that's what they want to waste their lives doing, let them. Just remember the best revenge is success, and a big part of success is having the guts to work to achieve your goals. So keep the target in sight, and maintain morale while you work to achieve your goals."

'Well, Kevin, I've been there, met them, been screwed around by a few, a very few, did all that. I've worked and wondered, and wavered, and I kept playing and kept writing. Then, last summer,

I returned to Vancouver to work as a studio musician. There's a lot of work here because of all the film and TV production. So I was off the bar circuit, still earning enough to feed myself, but best of all, I was around people who could help me get my songs to the right people, and I'm better than fed now!

'I wish I could report a wondrous overnight success, that I've had a breakthrough song that's sold millions. Well, I haven't, but three of my songs have been B tracks on two country albums and an album put out by one of those obscure San Francisco blues labels that only blues fans know about. And I was invited to play on all three albums, so I did sessions in Nashville, Los Angeles, and San Francisco, and I keep meeting and playing with people who like my stuff, and encourage me.

'Best of all Kevin, I have a life, and I'm a happy guy—all that, a positive bank balance, and even a wonderful woman in my life. I wish I could be there at the conference to tell you this personally, but I'll be in Nashville again. The sisters who recorded *River of Dreams* want me there to play when they record another one of my songs.

'Thanks for everything.

'Ron'

Kevin folded the letter and stuck it in his pocket. Before he could begin speaking again, the people in the audience were on their feet, applauding, stamping their feet, whistling. He grinned and waited for quiet.

"The letter seems like an appropriate note on which to close this conference," Kevin said when everyone was seated again. "Except, there's one other matter Danielle and I must take care of, and Kieron, we need you up here."

Kieron joined them, a puzzled look on his face. "You're supposed to close the show," he objected.

"Why, all this was your idea, the incubator, the program, the conference—" Kevin turned to the audience. "I think he's the one who deserves the applause."

Everyone stood clapping, shouting, stomping, whistling their agreement, and when they were done, Kieron made to move off stage.

"Whoa, brother, we aren't finished yet," Kevin said, as he pulled his brother back to the podium. "Danielle." He surrendered the lectern to her.

"Each year since the program started, Kevin has complained bitterly that after all the work we do together in the program, you folks face the nightmare of getting seed and start-up money out of the hands of those who control capital in this country," Danielle said. "So two years ago, Kevin and I put some people to work to deal with the problem, and today, we're finally ready to unveil our solution."

"We have travelled this country, arguing, coaxing, cajoling, twisting arms, shaming, blaming and doing everything necessary to squeeze money out of everyone we could convince to invest—except government—in a venture capital operation we created and call Big Chip Capital Corporation," Kevin said. "Danielle and our daughter Rachel went to collect the last of the papers from the lawyers yesterday, and we can now announce Big Chip has been capitalized at a little more than $30 million."

"The fund's mandate is to put 60 per cent of its holdings in blue-chip investments to provide a nominal return to investors, and to invest the other 40 per cent as seed capital in any reasonable business opportunity presented to its investment board," Danielle said. "But the charter provides that applicants from the Oswego incubator program go to the head of the line."

"But that's the only special consideration you'll get," Kevin said cheerfully. "*You* still have to sell your ideas to the board, and make money for *us,* your partners."

Kevin took the briefcase from Danielle and opened it up. Inside was a brass-bound gavel, which he held aloft. "At a charter shareholders' meeting conducted by computer and phone links, the shareholders unanimously agreed to offer chairmanship of Big Chip to Kieron Short, and I, as president of the corporation, have been authorized to ask if you will accept the post."

He held out the gavel to Kieron, who hesitated a moment, then took it. He took some time to roll it around in his hands, then smiled and turned to the audience. "I declare this conference closed," he said, tapping the lectern. "Now let's get to work! Let's do business!"

. . . .

1995: *Postscript*

Kevin and Danielle watched Rachel skip through the crowd as they walked through the auditorium. Their progress was slow, because people kept stopping them to shake hands, to comment on the weekend, or to speak about the closing talk.

This is good, Kevin thought. We're accomplishing something of value. He smiled as he recalled that he had doubted the incubator concept when Kieron first suggested it to him.

Well now—he turned to Danielle. "I'll be right back. There's something I have to take care of," he said, and kissed her cheek. He moved as quickly through the crowd as he could and caught Monique Pelletier and Jimmy Baldwin at the door.

"Monique. Jimmy. Do those invitations to speak with your people still stand?"

"Of course," Monique said. "We have different approaches, but we're still on the same side."

Kevin laughed. "Monique, don't try to sell a salesman. Push too hard, and you'll end up buying back your sale."

Monique pursed her lips, then smiled, and laughed. "I understand."

"You tell us when you're coming, and you can own the island," Jimmy said.

"Careful, Jimmy, I might end up doing that," Kevin chuckled. "I'll call you next week, when Danielle, Rachel and I have had a chance to catch up on each other, and we can set things up."

"Now don't assume you can change the country with one meeting in Ottawa," Monique said.

"Heavens, no, Monique," Kevin said with a smile. "That will take a little longer."

Monique stared at him, then began to laugh. They were all laughing when Danielle joined them.

"Private joke?" she asked.

Kevin took her hand, led her from the auditorium and said, "Well, it's like this..."

A Suggested Reading List

AUTHOR'S NOTE: We can always learn from other people, but which people can and should we learn from? There are many voices to hear, but only so many we can heed. The books listed below are a mix of older and newer works I've come to consult, or reread, to help me in my business, as the need arises. They do not include every book I've read about business, just some I didn't send to the recycler in frustration. Take what you can use. There are more out there waiting to be read. Good luck finding the ones that speak to you.

GENERAL REFERENCES
Alexander, Bevin, *How Great Generals Win,* Norton, 1993. ISBN 0-393-03531-X. The introduction offers up some germs of wisdom about translating thought into action.

Hawken, Paul, *The Next Economy,* Ballantine, 1983. ISBN 0-345-31392-5. An excellent essay on where our world is going, written before it was obvious that's where we were headed. Actually, anything he writes is worth reading. Also try Growing A Business.

CAREER PLANNING, SELF EVALUATION
Moses, Dr. Barbara, *The Career Planning Workbook,* BBM Human Resource Consultants, Inc., Toronto, Ontario, 1989. An excellent and comprehensive tool for self-evaluation and career planning that is pretty much a standard in the business. Copies are available only from BBM Human Resources Consultants of Toronto, or the company's associates in major North American cities. Phone BBM at 416-922-2455, or fax 902-2482.

COMMUNICATION SKILLS
Brill, Laura, *Business Writing Quick & Easy,* AMACOM, 1989. ISBN 0-8144-5979-X. An effective guide to effective writing.

Semmelmeyer, Madeline, and Bolander, Donald, *The Laurel Instant English Handbook*, Laurel, 1968. The book is described on the title page as, "An authoritative guide and reference on grammar, correct usage, and punctuation." An excellent choice of words.

FINANCE

Droms, William G., *Finance and Accounting for Nonfinancial Managers*, Addison Wesley, 1990. ISBN 0-201-52366-3. Skip the section on U.S. tax law, and learn about the accounting basics you need.

Zimmer, Henry B., *The Canadian Tax and Investment Guide*, McClelland & Stewart, 1993. ISBN 0-7710-90773. An excellent and invaluable reference on thinking about managing your money.

MANAGEMENT

Applegate, Jane, *Succeeding In Small Business*, Plume, 1992. ISBN 0-452-26886-9. A book about problem solving, with examples of problems and solutions other people have used. Best used as a guide, though, because situations and conditions rarely duplicate those encountered by others. Ignore the American tax and legal content.

Cohen, Herb, *You Can Negotiate Anything*, Bantam, 1983. ISBN 0-553-328109-7. Cohen's analysis of negotiation and illustration of its dynamics make this one of the best manuals on the art. Also available in a 1990 McLelland and Stewart edition, ISBN 1-55927-045-4.

Kaye, Harvey, *Decision Power*, Prentice Hall, 1992. ISBN 0-13-203548-0. A good guide that helps us understand about indecision, and getting past dithering and procrastination.

Kennedy, Dan, *The Ultimate No B.S., No Holds Barred, Kick Butt, Take No Prisoners, and Make Tons of Money Business Success Book*, Self Counsel Press, 1993. ISBN 0-88908-278-2. The book is nowhere near as bloodthirsty as its title, but it does discuss business, attitude, and the business perspective, in a clear, thoughtful, sensible manner.

Kishel, Gregory F. and Kishel, Patricia Gunter, *How To Start, Run, and Stay in Business*, Wiley, 1993. ISBN 0-471-59255-2. American content, particularly about laws, taxes, and finance, doesn't apply in Canada, but a nice supply of lists, tips, and to-dos that do apply here.

Morita, Akio, *Made In Japan,* Akio Morita and SONY, Dutton, 1986. ISBN 0-525-24465-4. A rare, frank autobiographical chronicle about building a major corporation from nothing.

Musashi, Miyamoto, *The Book of Five Rings, The Real Art of Japanese Management,* Bantam, 1982. It reads like dialogue from a martial arts movie, and takes some reading to fathom, but it teaches the essence of self-discipline, thought and application.

Pater, Robert, *Martial Arts And The Art Of Management,* Destiny Books, 1988. ISBN 0-89281-155-2. The subtitle—Strategies For Creativity Power & Control—is a good summary of what the book is about. (Also helps in the MOTIVATION AND SELF DISCIPLINE department.)

Tzu, Sun, *The Art of War,* translated by Samuel B. Griffith, Galaxy (Oxford University Press), 1963. ISBN 0-19-501476-6. Another important work on organization of thought and application of thought to action.

Walton, Sam, with John Huey, *Made In America,* Doubleday, 1992. ISBN 0-385-42615-1/46847-4/46860-1. An accessible, folksy primer on the retail business with ideas that touch on all aspects of business.

Winter, Barbara J., *Making A Living Without A Job,* Bantam, 1993. ISBN 0-553-37165-7. A touch sugar sweet on the motivational side, and quite American in content, but with good tips and guides.

MOTIVATION, SELF-DISCIPLINE, SUCCESS
Alexander, Colonel John B. U.S. Army (Ret), Groller, Major Richard, U.S. Army Reserve, Morris, Janet, *The Warrior's Edge,* 1990. ISBN 0-688-08889-9. A book about enhancing personal performance.

Kornfield, Jack, *Buddha's Little Instruction Book,* Bantam, 1994. ISBN 0-553-37385-4. Thoughts to ponder that can help clear the mind and focus energy and creativity.

Brown Jr., H. Jackson
1) *Life's Little Instruction Book,* Volumes One (1991) and Two (1993), Rutledge Hill. ISBN 1-55853-102-5 and 1-55853-216-1.
2) *Live And Learn And Pass It On,* Rutledge Hill, 1992. ISBN 1-55853-156-4.

Covey, Stephen R., *Principle-Centred Leadership,* Summit, 1991. ISBN 0-671-74910-2. A good guide to becoming a more effective individual and businessperson.

McWilliams, John-Roger and Peter, *The Portable DO IT!,* Prelude Press, 1993, ISBN 0-931580-81-1. Motivational thoughts.

ORGANIZATION
Kanarek, Lisa, *Organizing Your Home Office For Success,* Plume, 1993. ISBN 0-452-26833-8. An excellent resource.

Peacock, William E., *Corporate Combat, Military Strategies That Win Business Wars,* Berkley Non-fiction, 1984. ISBN 0-425-09110-4. The author stretches sometimes to validate his analogy of business competition to war, but tucked away in the information he uses are excellent lessons and ideas about focus.

Silver, Susan, *Organized To Be The Best,* Adams-Hall, 1989. ISBN 0-944708-23-4. A 411-page encyclopedia of organizational tips, ideas, charts and such. A bit overwhelming at times, but a good guide.

WORLD-VIEWS AND PERSONAL PORTRAITS
Gardner, John, *On Becoming a Novelist,* Harper & Row, 1983. ISBN 0-06-014956-6. An excellent book that, in general, speaks eloquently about the need for, and rewards that come of, understanding self, particularly in part one.

HUSTLING FOR A BUCK

"Some of us dream of being our own boss and some of us have no other option as the workaday world unravels. From home office to running an international manufacturing and marketing concern— why not think big? Hustling For A Buck takes you step-by-step through the demands of business. Dave Greber's critical analysis of each field of opportunity will help you find your path to success."

Michael Kane, Money Columnist
The Vancouver Sun

"Hustling For A Buck gives a unique insight on what it's like to be self-employed in Canada. For those who disdain dry theory, it covers the arts and skills of entrepreneurship in clear, conversational style."

Ted Mallett, Senior Economist,
Canadian Federation of Independent Business

"Dave Greber addresses a lot of meaty issues for the start-up entrepreneur using narrative featuring an engaging cast of characters."

Ellen Roseman, Money Editor,
Globe and Mail Report On Business

"Engaging, entertaining and motivating. I recommend it to all champions and practitioners of self-employment and entrepreneurship."

Bill Kaufmann, General Manager,
Calgary Chamber of Commerce

"Dave Greber addresses the fears and anxieties familiar to everyone who has ever sought success as an entrepreneur. His innovative and practical book is 'right on' with the 'right stuff'."

Joan Hill, President,
Core Consulting Inc., Toronto,
management consultants

"The book cleverly meshes the thoughts of its fictional entre- preneurs with real business examples and principles. In the process, it goes beyond the mush of 'dream and grow rich' to encourage practical responses and accelerate business savvy. By encouraging new businesses and enhanced management skills, Hustling For A Buck should produce some excellent spin-offs to society."

Robert A. Schultz Ph.D.,
Professor of Management, University of Calgary,
First Recipient, Order of the University of Calgary,
Coach of the perennially victorious
U of C Intercollegiate Business Competition Team

TO MOM:
SALLY. DAVID. HARVEY. LORRAINE.
FOUR FOR FOUR.
BATTING A THOUSAND.